The Masonic Treasurer's Logbook

By Durane Carter

Published By:

Sword & Bolt Enterprises, Inc.

ISBN 979-8-9862165-1-5

The Masonic Treasurers Logbook

Lodge:
_____

District: _____

Jurisdiction: _____

Start Date: _____

End Date: _____

Treasurer: _____

Assistant Treasurer: _____

Worshipful Master: _____

Contents

The Treasurer of the Lodge

The symbol of this stations is that of the Crossed Keys as the Treasurer is holds the keys to The Lodges funds.

The Treasurer is to tend the Lodge finances. They must receive all monies paid to the Lodge from the Secretary and provide a receipt to the secretary for said funds. Further they are to keep a just and regular account of the lodge's finances from the time custody of said funds are claimed. Lastly, they are to pay out any funds necessary when instructed by the Worshipful Master with the consent of the Lodge.

The Treasurers Station is one of masonic knowledge and experience. It requires that its holder know the workings of the lodge and be one that can maintain detailed records and organization. The Treasures duties will require them to handle the Lodge finances and transactions, pay all debts and render reports when required, as well as other reasonable duties that may be called upon them.

The Secretary's Station does not need to be in possession of an accounting degree. But should when possible be versed in managing finances, bookkeeping, and accounting. The Treasurer must also be well versed in their lodges bylaws as well as those of their jurisdictions.

The Treasurers Station is not one to be taken lightly nor should any station the members of a lodge entrust to one of its members. The affairs of a lodge require the attentive service and attention to detail of its Treasurer and just recording by its Treasurer. Use this tool and serve well.

Order of Business

Ritual Opening

Roll Call of Officers

Presentation of Lodge Agenda by the Worshipful Master

Reading and Approval of the Last Meetings Minutes

Treasurer Report

Committee Reports

Old Business

New Business

Reading and Referring of Petitions

Balloting of Candidates

Conferring of Degrees

Unfinished or Remaining Lawful Lodge Business

Reading of the Rough Minutes

Treasurers Report

Ritual Closing

Lodge: _____   **Date:** _____

1ˢᵗ Lodge Meeting

Time of Opening: _____

Roll Call of Officers   *List the present Officer, Assistant Officer Acting Officer (with "Acting" by their name) and Visiting Brothers names.*

Worshipful Master: _____

Senior Warden: _____

Junior Warden: _____

Secretary: _____

Treasurer: _____

Senior Deacon: _____

Junior Deacon: _____

Senior Steward: _____

Junior Steward: _____

Marshal: _____

Chaplain: _____

Tyler: _____

Visiting Brothers: _____

_____

_____

_____

_____

_____

_____

_____

_____

_____

_____

_____

_____

_____

_____

_____

_____

_____

_____

_____

_____

Lodge: _____ **Date:** _____

Reading and Approval of Minutes: *Document finance related adjustments or corrections to the minutes.*

_____
_____
_____
_____
_____
_____
_____
_____
_____
_____
_____
_____
_____
_____
_____
_____
_____
_____

Treasurer Report: *In this section list the Previous Meeting Account Balance, Deposits Received, Account Debits, Current Account Balance, and Outstanding Checks.*

Current Account Balance: _____

_____
_____
_____
_____
_____
_____
_____
_____
_____
_____
_____
_____
_____
_____
_____
_____
_____
_____
_____
_____

Lodge: _____   **Date:** _____

Funds Received: *In the section document all funds received from the Secretary and in what forms they were received. Example: 03 Checks: Check #'s 1123 for $100.00, 1134 for $250.00 and 2235 for $150.00, Total Checks $500.00. Total Cash Received: $250.00. Total Electronic Payments Received (verified in your service provider): $150.00. Grand Total Received: $900.00.*

_____
_____
_____
_____
_____
_____
_____
_____
_____
_____
_____
_____
_____
_____
_____
_____
_____
_____
_____
_____
_____
_____
_____
_____
_____
_____
_____
_____
_____
_____
_____
_____
_____
_____
_____
_____
_____
_____
_____

Lodge: _____ **Date:** _____

Funds Received *(Continued):* _____

_____
_____
_____
_____
_____
_____
_____
_____
_____
_____
_____
_____
_____
_____
_____
_____
_____
_____
_____
_____
_____
_____
_____
_____
_____
_____
_____
_____
_____
_____
_____
_____
_____
_____
_____
_____
_____
_____
_____

Lodge: _____ **Date:** _____

Funds Received *(Continued)*: _____

_____
_____
_____
_____
_____
_____
_____
_____
_____
_____
_____
_____
_____
_____
_____
_____
_____
_____
_____
_____
_____
_____
_____
_____
_____
_____
_____
_____
_____
_____
_____
_____
_____
_____
_____
_____
_____
_____
_____
_____
_____

Lodge: _____   **Date:** _____

Debits and Checks Dispersed: _Document all outgoing payments, the amount and method of_
disbursement as well as the receiver. (Including check and transaction numbers)

Lodge: _____   **Date:** _____

Debits and Checks Dispersed: *(Continued)*   _____

_____

_____

_____

_____

_____

_____

_____

_____

_____

_____

_____

_____

_____

_____

_____

_____

_____

_____

_____

_____

_____

_____

_____

_____

_____

_____

_____

_____

_____

_____

_____

_____

_____

_____

_____

_____

_____

Lodge: _____ **Date:** _____

Debits and Checks Dispersed: *(Continued)*

_____
_____
_____
_____
_____
_____
_____
_____
_____
_____
_____
_____
_____
_____
_____
_____
_____
_____
_____
_____
_____
_____
_____
_____
_____
_____
_____
_____
_____
_____
_____
_____
_____
_____
_____
_____
_____
_____
_____
_____
_____

Lodge: _____   **Date:** _____

Reading of the Rough Minutes: *Document finance related adjustments or corrections to the minutes.*

_____
_____
_____
_____
_____
_____
_____
_____
_____
_____
_____
_____
_____
_____
_____
_____
_____
_____

Treasurer Report: *In this section write a summary of financial transaction that transpired in the meeting. Example: Total funds received from the Secretary and Checks Written.*

Current Account Balance: _____

_____
_____
_____
_____
_____
_____
_____
_____
_____
_____
_____
_____
_____
_____
_____
_____
_____

Lodge: _____ **Date:** _____

Notes: _____

_____
_____
_____
_____
_____
_____
_____
_____
_____
_____
_____
_____
_____
_____
_____
_____
_____
_____
_____
_____
_____
_____
_____
_____
_____
_____
_____
_____
_____
_____
_____
_____
_____
_____
_____
_____
_____
_____
_____
_____
_____
_____

Lodge: _____ **Date:** _____

Notes: _____

_____

_____

_____

_____

_____

_____

_____

_____

_____

_____

_____

_____

_____

_____

_____

_____

_____

_____

_____

_____

_____

_____

_____

_____

_____

_____

_____

_____

_____

_____

_____

_____

_____

_____

_____

_____

_____

_____

_____

_____

_____

_____

Lodge: _____   **Date:** _____

Secretary & Treasurer Financial Reconciliation: *The Secretary and Treasurer will write a short summary of all funds received into the lodge by the Secretary and turned over to the Treasurer during the meeting in both books.*

_____
_____
_____
_____
_____
_____
_____
_____
_____
_____
_____
_____
_____
_____
_____
_____
_____
_____
_____
_____
_____
_____
_____

Secretary's Signature: _____
Treasurers Signature: _____
Worshipful Masters Signature: _____

Audit Team Notes: _____
_____
_____
_____
_____
_____
_____
_____
_____
_____

Audit Team Signature: _____
Audit Team Signature: _____
Audit Team Signature: _____

Lodge: _____   **Date:** _____

2ⁿᵈ Lodge Meeting

Time of Opening: _____

Roll Call of Officers   *List the present Officer, Assistant Officer Acting Officer (with "Acting" by their name) and Visiting Brothers names.*

Worshipful Master: _____
Senior Warden: _____
Junior Warden: _____
Secretary: _____
Treasurer: _____
Senior Deacon: _____
Junior Deacon: _____
Senior Steward: _____
Junior Steward: _____
Marshal: _____
Chaplain: _____
Tyler: _____

Visiting Brothers: _____
_____
_____
_____
_____
_____
_____
_____
_____
_____
_____
_____
_____
_____
_____
_____
_____
_____
_____
_____
_____
_____
_____
_____

Lodge: _____ **Date:** _____

Reading and Approval of Minutes: *Document finance related adjustments or corrections to the minutes.*

_____
_____
_____
_____
_____
_____
_____
_____
_____
_____
_____
_____
_____
_____
_____
_____
_____
_____

Treasurer Report: *In this section list the Previous Meeting Account Balance, Deposits Received, Account Debits, Current Account Balance, and Outstanding Checks.*

Current Account Balance: _____

_____
_____
_____
_____
_____
_____
_____
_____
_____
_____
_____
_____
_____
_____
_____
_____
_____
_____

Lodge: _____   **Date:** _____

Funds Received: *In the section document all funds received from the Secretary and in what forms they were received. Example: 03 Checks: Check #'s 1123 for $100.00, 1134 for $250.00 and 2235 for $150.00, Total Checks $500.00. Total Cash Received: $250.00. Total Electronic Payments Received (verified in your service provider): $150.00. Grand Total Received: $900.00.*

_____
_____
_____
_____
_____
_____
_____
_____
_____
_____
_____
_____
_____
_____
_____
_____
_____
_____
_____
_____
_____
_____
_____
_____
_____
_____
_____
_____
_____
_____
_____
_____
_____
_____
_____
_____
_____
_____
_____
_____

Lodge: _____ **Date:** _____

Funds Received *(Continued):* _____

_____

_____

_____

_____

_____

_____

_____

_____

_____

_____

_____

_____

_____

_____

_____

_____

_____

_____

_____

_____

_____

_____

_____

_____

_____

_____

_____

_____

_____

_____

_____

_____

_____

_____

_____

_____

_____

_____

_____

_____

_____

_____

Lodge: _____ **Date:** _____

Funds Received *(Continued)*: _____

_____

_____

_____

_____

_____

_____

_____

_____

_____

_____

_____

_____

_____

_____

_____

_____

_____

_____

_____

_____

_____

_____

_____

_____

_____

_____

_____

_____

_____

Lodge: _____ **Date:** _____

Debits and Checks Dispersed: _Document all outgoing payments, the amount and method of disbursement as well as the receiver. (Including check and transaction numbers)_

Lodge: _____ **Date:** _____

Debits and Checks Dispersed: *(Continued)* _____

Lodge: _____ **Date:** _____

Debits and Checks Dispersed: *(Continued)*

_____
_____
_____
_____
_____
_____
_____
_____
_____
_____
_____
_____
_____
_____
_____
_____
_____
_____
_____
_____
_____
_____
_____
_____
_____
_____
_____
_____
_____
_____
_____
_____
_____
_____
_____
_____
_____
_____
_____
_____
_____
_____

Lodge: _____ **Date:** _____

Reading of the Rough Minutes: *Document finance related adjustments or corrections to the minutes.*

_____
_____
_____
_____
_____
_____
_____
_____
_____
_____
_____
_____
_____
_____
_____
_____
_____
_____

Treasurer Report: *In this section write a summary of financial transaction that transpired in the meeting. Example: Total funds received from the Secretary and Checks Written.*

Current Account Balance: _____

_____
_____
_____
_____
_____
_____
_____
_____
_____
_____
_____
_____
_____
_____
_____
_____
_____
_____

Lodge: _____ **Date:** _____

Notes: _____

_____

_____

_____

_____

_____

_____

_____

_____

_____

_____

_____

_____

_____

_____

_____

_____

_____

_____

_____

_____

_____

_____

_____

_____

_____

_____

_____

_____

_____

_____

_____

_____

_____

_____

_____

_____

_____

_____

_____

_____

Lodge: _____   **Date:** _____

Notes: _____

_____

_____

_____

_____

_____

_____

_____

_____

_____

_____

_____

_____

_____

_____

_____

_____

_____

_____

_____

_____

_____

_____

_____

_____

_____

_____

_____

_____

_____

_____

_____

_____

_____

_____

_____

_____

_____

_____

_____

_____

_____

Lodge: _____ **Date:** _____

Secretary & Treasurer Financial Reconciliation: *The Secretary and Treasurer will write a short summary of all funds received into the lodge by the Secretary and turned over to the Treasurer during the meeting in both books.*

_____
_____
_____
_____
_____
_____
_____
_____
_____
_____
_____
_____
_____
_____
_____
_____
_____
_____
_____
_____
_____

Secretary's Signature: _____
Treasurers Signature: _____
Worshipful Masters Signature: _____

Audit Team Notes: _____

_____
_____
_____
_____
_____
_____
_____
_____
_____

Audit Team Signature: _____
Audit Team Signature: _____
Audit Team Signature: _____

Lodge: _____ **Date:** _____

3rd Lodge Meeting

Time of Opening: _____

Roll Call of Officers

List the present Officer, Assistant Officer Acting Officer (with "Acting" by their name) and Visiting Brothers names.

Worshipful Master: _____

Senior Warden: _____

Junior Warden: _____

Secretary: _____

Treasurer: _____

Senior Deacon: _____

Junior Deacon: _____

Senior Steward: _____

Junior Steward: _____

Marshal: _____

Chaplain: _____

Tyler: _____

Visiting Brothers: _____

_____

_____

_____

_____

_____

_____

_____

_____

_____

_____

_____

_____

_____

_____

_____

_____

_____

_____

_____

_____

_____

_____

Lodge: _____ **Date:** _____

Reading and Approval of Minutes: *Document finance related adjustments or corrections to the minutes.*

_____
_____
_____
_____
_____
_____
_____
_____
_____
_____
_____
_____
_____
_____
_____
_____

Treasurer Report: *In this section list the Previous Meeting Account Balance, Deposits Received, Account Debits, Current Account Balance, and Outstanding Checks.*

Current Account Balance: _____

_____
_____
_____
_____
_____
_____
_____
_____
_____
_____
_____
_____
_____
_____
_____
_____
_____

Lodge: _____   **Date:** _____

Funds Received: *In the section document all funds received from the Secretary and in what forms they were received. Example: 03 Checks: Check #'s 1123 for $100.00, 1134 for $250.00 and 2235 for $150.00, Total Checks $500.00. Total Cash Received: $250.00. Total Electronic Payments Received (verified in your service provider): $150.00. Grand Total Received: $900.00.*

Lodge: _____   **Date:** _____

Funds Received *(Continued)*:   _____

_____
_____
_____
_____
_____
_____
_____
_____
_____
_____
_____
_____
_____
_____
_____
_____
_____
_____
_____
_____
_____
_____
_____
_____
_____
_____
_____
_____
_____
_____
_____
_____
_____
_____

Lodge: _____ **Date:** _____

Funds Received *(Continued)*: _____

_____

_____

_____

_____

_____

_____

_____

_____

_____

_____

_____

_____

_____

_____

_____

_____

_____

_____

_____

_____

_____

_____

_____

_____

_____

_____

_____

_____

_____

_____

_____

_____

_____

_____

_____

_____

_____

_____

_____

_____

_____

_____

_____

_____

_____

Lodge: _____ **Date:** _____

Debits and Checks Dispersed: *Document all outgoing payments, the amount and method of* disbursement as well as the receiver. *(Including check and transaction numbers)*

_____
_____
_____
_____
_____
_____
_____
_____
_____
_____
_____
_____
_____
_____
_____
_____
_____
_____
_____
_____
_____
_____
_____
_____
_____
_____
_____
_____
_____
_____
_____
_____
_____
_____
_____
_____
_____
_____
_____
_____
_____
_____
_____
_____

Lodge: _____ **Date:** _____

Debits and Checks Dispersed: *(Continued)* _____

Lodge: _____ **Date:** _____

Debits and Checks Dispersed: *(Continued)*

Lodge: _____ **Date:** _____

Reading of the Rough Minutes: *Document finance related adjustments or corrections to the minutes.*

_____
_____
_____
_____
_____
_____
_____
_____
_____
_____
_____
_____
_____
_____
_____
_____
_____
_____
_____
_____

Treasurer Report: *In this section write a summary of financial transaction that transpired in the meeting. Example: Total funds received from the Secretary and Checks Written.*

Current Account Balance: _____

_____
_____
_____
_____
_____
_____
_____
_____
_____
_____
_____
_____
_____
_____
_____
_____
_____
_____

Lodge: _____ **Date:** _____

Notes: _____

_____

_____

_____

_____

_____

_____

_____

_____

_____

_____

_____

_____

_____

_____

_____

_____

_____

_____

_____

_____

_____

_____

_____

_____

_____

_____

_____

_____

_____

_____

_____

_____

_____

_____

_____

_____

_____

_____

_____

_____

_____

_____

_____

_____

_____

Lodge: _____ **Date:** _____

Notes: _____

_____
_____
_____
_____
_____
_____
_____
_____
_____
_____
_____
_____
_____
_____
_____
_____
_____
_____
_____
_____
_____
_____
_____
_____
_____
_____
_____
_____
_____
_____
_____
_____
_____
_____
_____
_____
_____
_____
_____
_____
_____

Lodge: _____   **Date:** _____

Secretary & Treasurer Financial Reconciliation: *The Secretary and Treasurer will write a short summary*
of all funds received into the lodge by the Secretary and turned over to the Treasurer during the meeting in both books.

_____
_____
_____
_____
_____
_____
_____
_____
_____
_____
_____
_____
_____
_____
_____
_____
_____
_____
_____
_____
_____
_____

Secretary's Signature: _____
Treasurers Signature: _____
Worshipful Masters Signature: _____

Audit Team Notes: _____
_____
_____
_____
_____
_____
_____
_____
_____
_____
_____
_____

Audit Team Signature: _____
Audit Team Signature: _____
Audit Team Signature: _____

Lodge: _____   **Date:** _____

4th Lodge Meeting

Time of Opening: _____

Roll Call of Officers   *List the present Officer, Assistant Officer Acting Officer (with "Acting" by their name) and Visiting Brothers names.*

Worshipful Master: _____
Senior Warden: _____
Junior Warden: _____
Secretary: _____
Treasurer: _____
Senior Deacon: _____
Junior Deacon: _____
Senior Steward: _____
Junior Steward: _____
Marshal: _____
Chaplain: _____
Tyler: _____

Visiting Brothers: _____
_____
_____
_____
_____
_____
_____
_____
_____
_____
_____
_____
_____
_____
_____
_____
_____
_____
_____
_____
_____
_____

Lodge: _____   **Date:** _____

Reading and Approval of Minutes: _Document finance related adjustments or corrections to the minutes._

_____
_____
_____
_____
_____
_____
_____
_____
_____
_____
_____
_____
_____
_____
_____
_____

Treasurer Report: _In this section list the Previous Meeting Account Balance, Deposits Received, Account Debits, Current Account Balance, and Outstanding Checks._

Current Account Balance: _____

_____
_____
_____
_____
_____
_____
_____
_____
_____
_____
_____
_____
_____
_____
_____
_____
_____
_____

Lodge: _____   **Date:** _____

Funds Received: *In the section document all funds received from the Secretary and in what forms they were received. Example: 03 Checks: Check #'s 1123 for $100.00, 1134 for $250.00 and 2235 for $150.00, Total Checks $500.00. Total Cash Received: $250.00. Total Electronic Payments Received (verified in your service provider): $150.00. Grand Total Received: $900.00.*

_____
_____
_____
_____
_____
_____
_____
_____
_____
_____
_____
_____
_____
_____
_____
_____
_____
_____
_____
_____
_____
_____
_____
_____
_____
_____
_____
_____
_____
_____
_____
_____
_____
_____
_____
_____
_____

Lodge: _____   **Date:** _____

Funds Received *(Continued):*   _____

_____
_____
_____
_____
_____
_____
_____
_____
_____
_____
_____
_____
_____
_____
_____
_____
_____
_____
_____
_____
_____
_____
_____
_____
_____
_____
_____
_____
_____
_____
_____
_____
_____
_____
_____
_____
_____
_____
_____
_____
_____

Lodge: _____   **Date:** _____

Funds Received *(Continued):*   _____

_____
_____
_____
_____
_____
_____
_____
_____
_____
_____
_____
_____
_____
_____
_____
_____
_____
_____
_____
_____
_____
_____
_____
_____
_____
_____
_____
_____
_____
_____
_____
_____
_____
_____
_____
_____
_____
_____
_____
_____
_____
_____
_____

Lodge: _____ **Date:** _____

Debits and Checks Dispersed: _Document all outgoing payments, the amount and method of_
disbursement as well as the receiver. (Including check and transaction numbers)

Lodge: _____ **Date:** _____

Debits and Checks Dispersed: *(Continued)* _____

_____
_____
_____
_____
_____
_____
_____
_____
_____
_____
_____
_____
_____
_____
_____
_____
_____
_____
_____
_____
_____
_____
_____
_____
_____
_____
_____
_____
_____
_____
_____
_____
_____
_____
_____
_____
_____
_____
_____
_____
_____
_____
_____
_____
_____
_____

Lodge: _____ **Date:** _____

Debits and Checks Dispersed: *(Continued)*

Lodge: _____ **Date:** _____

Reading of the Rough Minutes: *Document finance related adjustments or corrections to the minutes.*

_____
_____
_____
_____
_____
_____
_____
_____
_____
_____
_____
_____
_____
_____
_____
_____
_____
_____
_____
_____

Treasurer Report: *In this section write a summary of financial transaction that transpired in the meeting. Example: Total funds received from the Secretary and Checks Written.*

Current Account Balance: _____

_____
_____
_____
_____
_____
_____
_____
_____
_____
_____
_____
_____
_____
_____
_____
_____
_____
_____
_____
_____

Lodge: _____ **Date:** _____

Notes: _____

_____

_____

_____

_____

_____

_____

_____

_____

_____

_____

_____

_____

_____

_____

_____

_____

_____

_____

_____

_____

_____

_____

_____

_____

_____

_____

_____

_____

_____

_____

_____

_____

_____

_____

_____

_____

_____

_____

_____

_____

_____

_____

_____

_____

_____

Lodge: _____ **Date:** _____

Notes: _____

_____

Lodge: _____ **Date:** _____

Secretary & Treasurer Financial Reconciliation: *The Secretary and Treasurer will write a short summary of all funds received into the lodge by the Secretary and turned over to the Treasurer during the meeting in both books.*

_____
_____
_____
_____
_____
_____
_____
_____
_____
_____
_____
_____
_____
_____
_____
_____
_____
_____
_____
_____
_____
_____

Secretary's Signature: _____
Treasurers Signature: _____
Worshipful Masters Signature: _____

Audit Team Notes: _____
_____
_____
_____
_____
_____
_____
_____
_____
_____
_____
_____

Audit Team Signature: _____
Audit Team Signature: _____
Audit Team Signature: _____

Lodge: _____   **Date:** _____

5th Lodge Meeting

Time of Opening: _____

Roll Call of Officers   *List the present Officer, Assistant Officer Acting Officer (with "Acting" by their name) and Visiting Brothers names.*

Worshipful Master: _____
Senior Warden: _____
Junior Warden: _____
Secretary: _____
Treasurer: _____
Senior Deacon: _____
Junior Deacon: _____
Senior Steward: _____
Junior Steward: _____
Marshal: _____
Chaplain: _____
Tyler: _____

Visiting Brothers: _____
_____
_____
_____
_____
_____
_____
_____
_____
_____
_____
_____
_____
_____
_____
_____
_____
_____
_____
_____
_____
_____
_____

Lodge: _____   **Date:** _____

Reading and Approval of Minutes: _Document finance related adjustments or corrections to the minutes._

_____
_____
_____
_____
_____
_____
_____
_____
_____
_____
_____
_____
_____
_____
_____
_____

Treasurer Report: _In this section list the Previous Meeting Account Balance, Deposits Received, Account Debits, Current Account Balance, and Outstanding Checks._

Current Account Balance: _____

_____
_____
_____
_____
_____
_____
_____
_____
_____
_____
_____
_____
_____
_____
_____
_____
_____

Lodge: _____ **Date:** _____

Funds Received: *In the section document all funds received from the Secretary and in what forms they were received. Example: 03 Checks: Check #'s 1123 for $100.00, 1134 for $250.00 and 2235 for $150.00, Total Checks $500.00. Total Cash Received: $250.00. Total Electronic Payments Received (verified in your service provider): $150.00. Grand Total Received: $900.00.*

_____

_____

_____

_____

_____

_____

_____

_____

_____

_____

_____

_____

_____

_____

_____

_____

_____

_____

_____

_____

_____

_____

_____

_____

_____

_____

_____

_____

_____

_____

_____

_____

_____

_____

_____

_____

_____

_____

_____

Lodge: _____ **Date:** _____

Funds Received *(Continued)*: _____

_____
_____
_____
_____
_____
_____
_____
_____
_____
_____
_____
_____
_____
_____
_____
_____
_____
_____
_____
_____
_____
_____
_____
_____
_____
_____
_____
_____
_____
_____
_____
_____
_____
_____
_____
_____
_____
_____
_____
_____
_____
_____
_____

Lodge: _____ **Date:** _____

Funds Received *(Continued):* _____

_____

_____

_____

_____

_____

_____

_____

_____

_____

_____

_____

_____

_____

_____

_____

_____

_____

_____

_____

_____

_____

_____

_____

_____

_____

_____

_____

_____

_____

_____

_____

_____

_____

_____

_____

_____

_____

_____

_____

_____

_____

_____

Lodge: _____ **Date:** _____

Debits and Checks Dispersed: _Document all outgoing payments, the amount and method of disbursement as well as the receiver. (Including check and transaction numbers)_

Lodge: _____ **Date:** _____

Debits and Checks Dispersed: *(Continued)* _____

_____
_____
_____
_____
_____
_____
_____
_____
_____
_____
_____
_____
_____
_____
_____
_____
_____
_____
_____
_____
_____
_____
_____
_____
_____
_____
_____
_____
_____
_____
_____
_____
_____
_____
_____
_____
_____
_____
_____

Lodge: _____   **Date:** _____

Debits and Checks Dispersed: *(Continued)*

Lodge: _____   **Date:** _____

Reading of the Rough Minutes: *Document finance related adjustments or corrections to the minutes.*

_____
_____
_____
_____
_____
_____
_____
_____
_____
_____
_____
_____
_____
_____
_____
_____
_____
_____

Treasurer Report: *In this section write a summary of financial transaction that transpired in the meeting. Example: Total funds received from the Secretary and Checks Written.*

Current Account Balance: _____

_____
_____
_____
_____
_____
_____
_____
_____
_____
_____
_____
_____
_____
_____
_____
_____
_____
_____

Lodge: _____ **Date:** _____

Notes: _____

_____
_____
_____
_____
_____
_____
_____
_____
_____
_____
_____
_____
_____
_____
_____
_____
_____
_____
_____
_____
_____
_____
_____
_____
_____
_____
_____
_____
_____
_____
_____
_____
_____
_____
_____
_____
_____
_____
_____
_____
_____
_____
_____
_____
_____

Lodge: _____ **Date:** _____

Notes: _____

_____
_____
_____
_____
_____
_____
_____
_____
_____
_____
_____
_____
_____
_____
_____
_____
_____
_____
_____
_____
_____
_____
_____
_____
_____
_____
_____
_____
_____
_____
_____
_____
_____
_____
_____
_____
_____
_____
_____

Lodge: _____ **Date:** _____

Secretary & Treasurer Financial Reconciliation: *The Secretary and Treasurer will write a short summary of all funds received into the lodge by the Secretary and turned over to the Treasurer during the meeting in both books.*

_____

_____

_____

_____

_____

_____

_____

_____

_____

_____

_____

_____

_____

_____

_____

_____

_____

_____

_____

_____

_____

Secretary's Signature: _____

Treasurers Signature: _____

Worshipful Masters Signature: _____

Audit Team Notes: _____

_____

_____

_____

_____

_____

_____

_____

_____

_____

_____

Audit Team Signature: _____

Audit Team Signature: _____

Audit Team Signature: _____

Lodge: _____   **Date:** _____

6ᵗʰ Lodge Meeting

Time of Opening: _____

Roll Call of Officers   *List the present Officer, Assistant Officer Acting Officer (with "Acting" by their name) and Visiting Brothers names.*

Worshipful Master: _____
Senior Warden: _____
Junior Warden: _____
Secretary: _____
Treasurer: _____
Senior Deacon: _____
Junior Deacon: _____
Senior Steward: _____
Junior Steward: _____
Marshal: _____
Chaplain: _____
Tyler: _____

Visiting Brothers: _____
_____
_____
_____
_____
_____
_____
_____
_____
_____
_____
_____
_____
_____
_____
_____
_____
_____
_____
_____
_____

Lodge: _____   **Date:** _____

Reading and Approval of Minutes: *Document finance related adjustments or corrections to the minutes.*

_____
_____
_____
_____
_____
_____
_____
_____
_____
_____
_____
_____
_____
_____
_____
_____
_____
_____

Treasurer Report: *In this section list the Previous Meeting Account Balance, Deposits Received, Account Debits, Current Account Balance, and Outstanding Checks.*

Current Account Balance: _____

_____
_____
_____
_____
_____
_____
_____
_____
_____
_____
_____
_____
_____
_____
_____
_____
_____

Lodge: _____   **Date:** _____

Funds Received: *In the section document all funds received from the Secretary and in what forms they were received. Example: 03 Checks: Check #'s 1123 for $100.00, 1134 for $250.00 and 2235 for $150.00, Total Checks $500.00. Total Cash Received: $250.00. Total Electronic Payments Received (verified in your service provider): $150.00. Grand Total Received: $900.00.*

_____
_____
_____
_____
_____
_____
_____
_____
_____
_____
_____
_____
_____
_____
_____
_____
_____
_____
_____
_____
_____
_____
_____
_____
_____
_____
_____
_____
_____
_____
_____
_____
_____
_____
_____
_____
_____

Lodge: _____ **Date:** _____

Funds Received *(Continued)*: _____

_____
_____
_____
_____
_____
_____
_____
_____
_____
_____
_____
_____
_____
_____
_____
_____
_____
_____
_____
_____
_____
_____
_____
_____
_____
_____
_____
_____
_____
_____
_____
_____
_____
_____
_____
_____
_____
_____
_____
_____

Lodge: _____ **Date:** _____

Funds Received *(Continued):* _____

_____
_____
_____
_____
_____
_____
_____
_____
_____
_____
_____
_____
_____
_____
_____
_____
_____
_____
_____
_____
_____
_____
_____
_____
_____
_____
_____
_____
_____
_____
_____
_____
_____
_____
_____
_____
_____
_____
_____
_____
_____
_____

Lodge: _____   **Date:** _____

Debits and Checks Dispersed: _Document all outgoing payments, the amount and method of_
disbursement as well as the receiver. (Including check and transaction numbers)

_____
_____
_____
_____
_____
_____
_____
_____
_____
_____
_____
_____
_____
_____
_____
_____
_____
_____
_____
_____
_____
_____
_____
_____
_____
_____
_____
_____
_____
_____
_____
_____
_____
_____
_____
_____
_____
_____
_____

Lodge: _____ **Date:** _____

Debits and Checks Dispersed: *(Continued)* _____

_____
_____
_____
_____
_____
_____
_____
_____
_____
_____
_____
_____
_____
_____
_____
_____
_____
_____
_____
_____
_____
_____
_____
_____
_____
_____
_____
_____
_____
_____
_____
_____
_____
_____
_____
_____
_____
_____
_____
_____
_____
_____
_____
_____

Lodge: _____ **Date:** _____

Debits and Checks Dispersed: *(Continued)*

Lodge: _____   **Date:** _____

Reading of the Rough Minutes: *Document finance related adjustments or corrections to the minutes.*

_____
_____
_____
_____
_____
_____
_____
_____
_____
_____
_____
_____
_____
_____
_____
_____
_____
_____
_____
_____
_____

Treasurer Report: *In this section write a summary of financial transaction that transpired in the meeting. Example: Total funds received from the Secretary and Checks Written.*

Current Account Balance: _____

_____
_____
_____
_____
_____
_____
_____
_____
_____
_____
_____
_____
_____
_____
_____
_____
_____
_____
_____
_____

Lodge: _____ **Date:** _____

Notes: _____

_____
_____
_____
_____
_____
_____
_____
_____
_____
_____
_____
_____
_____
_____
_____
_____
_____
_____
_____
_____
_____
_____
_____
_____
_____
_____
_____
_____
_____
_____
_____
_____
_____
_____
_____
_____
_____
_____
_____
_____
_____
_____

Lodge: _____ **Date:** _____

Notes: _____

_____

_____

_____

_____

_____

_____

_____

_____

_____

_____

_____

_____

_____

_____

_____

_____

_____

_____

_____

_____

_____

_____

_____

_____

_____

_____

_____

_____

_____

_____

_____

_____

_____

_____

_____

_____

_____

_____

_____

Lodge: _____ **Date:** _____

Secretary & Treasurer Financial Reconciliation: *The Secretary and Treasurer will write a short summary*
of all funds received into the lodge by the Secretary and turned over to the Treasurer during the meeting in both books.

_____
_____
_____
_____
_____
_____
_____
_____
_____
_____
_____
_____
_____
_____
_____
_____
_____
_____
_____
_____
_____
_____

Secretary's Signature: _____
Treasurers Signature: _____
Worshipful Masters Signature: _____

Audit Team Notes: _____
_____
_____
_____
_____
_____
_____
_____
_____
_____
_____

Audit Team Signature: _____
Audit Team Signature: _____
Audit Team Signature: _____

Lodge: _____   **Date:** _____

7th Lodge Meeting

Time of Opening: _____

Roll Call of Officers   *List the present Officer, Assistant Officer Acting Officer (with "Acting" by their name) and Visiting Brothers names.*

Worshipful Master: _____

Senior Warden: _____

Junior Warden: _____

Secretary: _____

Treasurer: _____

Senior Deacon: _____

Junior Deacon: _____

Senior Steward: _____

Junior Steward: _____

Marshal: _____

Chaplain: _____

Tyler: _____

Visiting Brothers: _____

_____

_____

_____

_____

_____

_____

_____

_____

_____

_____

_____

_____

_____

_____

_____

_____

_____

_____

_____

_____

_____

_____

_____

Lodge: _____ **Date:** _____

Reading and Approval of Minutes: *Document finance related adjustments or corrections to the minutes.*

_____

_____

_____

_____

_____

_____

_____

_____

_____

_____

_____

_____

_____

_____

_____

_____

_____

Treasurer Report: *In this section list the Previous Meeting Account Balance, Deposits Received, Account Debits, Current Account Balance, and Outstanding Checks.*

Current Account Balance: _____

_____

_____

_____

_____

_____

_____

_____

_____

_____

_____

_____

_____

_____

_____

_____

_____

_____

Lodge: _____   **Date:** _____

Funds Received: _In the section document all funds received from the Secretary and in what forms they were received. Example: 03 Checks: Check #'s 1123 for $100.00, 1134 for $250.00 and 2235 for $150.00, Total Checks $500.00. Total Cash Received: $250.00. Total Electronic Payments Received (verified in your service provider): $150.00. Grand Total Received: $900.00._

Lodge: _____ **Date:** _____

Funds Received *(Continued):* _____

_____
_____
_____
_____
_____
_____
_____
_____
_____
_____
_____
_____
_____
_____
_____
_____
_____
_____
_____
_____
_____
_____
_____
_____
_____
_____
_____
_____
_____
_____
_____
_____
_____
_____
_____
_____
_____
_____
_____
_____

Lodge: _____ **Date:** _____

Funds Received *(Continued):* _____

_____
_____
_____
_____
_____
_____
_____
_____
_____
_____
_____
_____
_____
_____
_____
_____
_____
_____
_____
_____
_____
_____
_____
_____
_____
_____
_____
_____
_____
_____
_____
_____
_____
_____
_____
_____
_____
_____
_____
_____
_____
_____

Lodge: _____   **Date:** _____

Debits and Checks Dispersed: _Document all outgoing payments, the amount and method of_
disbursement as well as the receiver. (Including check and transaction numbers)

Lodge: _____   **Date:** _____

Debits and Checks Dispersed: *(Continued)* _____

_____
_____
_____
_____
_____
_____
_____
_____
_____
_____
_____
_____
_____
_____
_____
_____
_____
_____
_____
_____
_____
_____
_____
_____
_____
_____
_____
_____
_____
_____
_____
_____
_____
_____
_____
_____
_____
_____
_____
_____

Lodge: _____   **Date:** _____

Debits and Checks Dispersed: *(Continued)*

Lodge: _____   **Date:** _____

Reading of the Rough Minutes: *Document finance related adjustments or corrections to the minutes.*

_____
_____
_____
_____
_____
_____
_____
_____
_____
_____
_____
_____
_____
_____
_____
_____
_____
_____
_____
_____

Treasurer Report: *In this section write a summary of financial transaction that transpired in the meeting. Example: Total funds received from the Secretary and Checks Written.*

Current Account Balance: _____

_____
_____
_____
_____
_____
_____
_____
_____
_____
_____
_____
_____
_____
_____
_____
_____
_____
_____
_____

Lodge: _____ **Date:** _____

Notes: _____

_____

_____

_____

_____

_____

_____

_____

_____

_____

_____

_____

_____

_____

_____

_____

_____

_____

_____

_____

_____

_____

_____

_____

_____

_____

_____

_____

_____

_____

_____

_____

_____

_____

_____

_____

_____

_____

_____

_____

_____

_____

_____

Lodge: _____   **Date:** _____

Notes: _____

_____
_____
_____
_____
_____
_____
_____
_____
_____
_____
_____
_____
_____
_____
_____
_____
_____
_____
_____
_____
_____
_____
_____
_____
_____
_____
_____
_____
_____
_____
_____
_____
_____
_____
_____
_____
_____
_____
_____

Lodge: _____ **Date:** _____

Secretary & Treasurer Financial Reconciliation: *The Secretary and Treasurer will write a short summary of all funds received into the lodge by the Secretary and turned over to the Treasurer during the meeting in both books.*

_____
_____
_____
_____
_____
_____
_____
_____
_____
_____
_____
_____
_____
_____
_____
_____
_____
_____
_____
_____
_____
_____
_____

Secretary's Signature: _____
Treasurers Signature: _____
Worshipful Masters Signature: _____

Audit Team Notes: _____
_____
_____
_____
_____
_____
_____
_____
_____
_____
_____

Audit Team Signature: _____
Audit Team Signature: _____
Audit Team Signature: _____

Lodge: _____   **Date:** _____

8th Lodge Meeting

Time of Opening: _____

Roll Call of Officers   *List the present Officer, Assistant Officer Acting Officer (with "Acting" by their name) and Visiting Brothers names.*

Worshipful Master: _____
Senior Warden: _____
Junior Warden: _____
Secretary: _____
Treasurer: _____
Senior Deacon: _____
Junior Deacon: _____
Senior Steward: _____
Junior Steward: _____
Marshal: _____
Chaplain: _____
Tyler: _____

Visiting Brothers: _____
_____
_____
_____
_____
_____
_____
_____
_____
_____
_____
_____
_____
_____
_____
_____
_____
_____
_____
_____
_____

Lodge: _____   **Date:** _____

Reading and Approval of Minutes: *Document finance related adjustments or corrections to the minutes.*

_____
_____
_____
_____
_____
_____
_____
_____
_____
_____
_____
_____
_____
_____
_____
_____

Treasurer Report: *In this section list the Previous Meeting Account Balance, Deposits Received, Account Debits, Current Account Balance, and Outstanding Checks.*

Current Account Balance: _____

_____
_____
_____
_____
_____
_____
_____
_____
_____
_____
_____
_____
_____
_____
_____
_____

Lodge: _____ **Date:** _____

Funds Received: *In the section document all funds received from the Secretary and in what forms they were received. Example: 03 Checks: Check #'s 1123 for $100.00, 1134 for $250.00 and 2235 for $150.00, Total Checks $500.00. Total Cash Received: $250.00. Total Electronic Payments Received (verified in your service provider): $150.00. Grand Total Received: $900.00.*

Lodge: _____ **Date:** _____

Funds Received *(Continued)*: _____

_____

_____

_____

_____

_____

_____

_____

_____

_____

_____

_____

_____

_____

_____

_____

_____

_____

_____

_____

_____

_____

_____

_____

_____

_____

_____

_____

_____

_____

_____

_____

_____

_____

_____

_____

_____

_____

_____

_____

_____

Lodge: _____ **Date:** _____

Funds Received *(Continued):* _____

_____
_____
_____
_____
_____
_____
_____
_____
_____
_____
_____
_____
_____
_____
_____
_____
_____
_____
_____
_____
_____
_____
_____
_____
_____
_____
_____
_____
_____
_____
_____
_____
_____
_____
_____
_____
_____
_____
_____
_____

Lodge: _____   **Date:** _____

Debits and Checks Dispersed: _Document all outgoing payments, the amount and method of_
disbursement as well as the receiver. (Including check and transaction numbers)

Lodge: _____   **Date:** _____

Debits and Checks Dispersed: *(Continued)*   _____

_____
_____
_____
_____
_____
_____
_____
_____
_____
_____
_____
_____
_____
_____
_____
_____
_____
_____
_____
_____
_____
_____
_____
_____
_____
_____
_____
_____
_____
_____
_____
_____
_____
_____
_____
_____
_____
_____
_____
_____
_____
_____
_____

Lodge: _____ **Date:** _____

Debits and Checks Dispersed: *(Continued)*

Lodge: _____   **Date:** _____

Reading of the Rough Minutes: *Document finance related adjustments or corrections to the minutes.*

_____
_____
_____
_____
_____
_____
_____
_____
_____
_____
_____
_____
_____
_____
_____
_____
_____
_____

Treasurer Report: *In this section write a summary of financial transaction that transpired in the meeting. Example: Total funds received from the Secretary and Checks Written.*

Current Account Balance: _____

_____
_____
_____
_____
_____
_____
_____
_____
_____
_____
_____
_____
_____
_____
_____
_____
_____
_____

Lodge: _____ **Date:** _____

Notes: _____

_____

_____

_____

_____

_____

_____

_____

_____

_____

_____

_____

_____

_____

_____

_____

_____

_____

_____

_____

_____

_____

_____

_____

_____

_____

_____

_____

_____

_____

_____

_____

_____

_____

_____

_____

_____

_____

_____

_____

_____

Lodge: _____ **Date:** _____

Notes: _____

_____

_____

_____

_____

_____

_____

_____

_____

_____

_____

_____

_____

_____

_____

_____

_____

_____

_____

_____

_____

_____

_____

_____

_____

_____

_____

_____

_____

_____

_____

_____

_____

_____

_____

_____

_____

_____

_____

_____

_____

Lodge: _____   **Date:** _____

Secretary & Treasurer Financial Reconciliation: *The Secretary and Treasurer will write a short summary*
of all funds received into the lodge by the Secretary and turned over to the Treasurer during the meeting in both books.

_____
_____
_____
_____
_____
_____
_____
_____
_____
_____
_____
_____
_____
_____
_____
_____
_____
_____
_____
_____
_____
_____

Secretary's Signature: _____
Treasurers Signature: _____
Worshipful Masters Signature: _____

Audit Team Notes: _____
_____
_____
_____
_____
_____
_____
_____
_____
_____
_____

Audit Team Signature: _____
Audit Team Signature: _____
Audit Team Signature: _____

Lodge: _____   **Date:** _____

9th Lodge Meeting

Time of Opening: _____

Roll Call of Officers   *List the present Officer, Assistant Officer Acting Officer (with "Acting" by their name) and Visiting Brothers names.*

Worshipful Master: _____

Senior Warden: _____

Junior Warden: _____

Secretary: _____

Treasurer: _____

Senior Deacon: _____

Junior Deacon: _____

Senior Steward: _____

Junior Steward: _____

Marshal: _____

Chaplain: _____

Tyler: _____

Visiting Brothers: _____

_____

_____

_____

_____

_____

_____

_____

_____

_____

_____

_____

_____

_____

_____

_____

_____

_____

_____

_____

_____

_____

_____

Lodge: _____ **Date:** _____

Reading and Approval of Minutes: *Document finance related adjustments or corrections to the minutes.*

_____
_____
_____
_____
_____
_____
_____
_____
_____
_____
_____
_____
_____
_____
_____
_____
_____

Treasurer Report: *In this section list the Previous Meeting Account Balance, Deposits Received, Account Debits, Current Account Balance, and Outstanding Checks.*

Current Account Balance: _____

_____
_____
_____
_____
_____
_____
_____
_____
_____
_____
_____
_____
_____
_____
_____
_____
_____
_____

Lodge: _____   **Date:** _____

Funds Received: *In the section document all funds received from the Secretary and in what forms they were received. Example: 03 Checks: Check #'s 1123 for $100.00, 1134 for $250.00 and 2235 for $150.00, Total Checks $500.00. Total Cash Received: $250.00. Total Electronic Payments Received (verified in your service provider): $150.00. Grand Total Received: $900.00.*

Lodge: _____   **Date:** _____

Funds Received *(Continued)*:   _____

_____
_____
_____
_____
_____
_____
_____
_____
_____
_____
_____
_____
_____
_____
_____
_____
_____
_____
_____
_____
_____
_____
_____
_____
_____
_____
_____
_____
_____
_____
_____
_____
_____
_____
_____
_____
_____
_____
_____
_____
_____

Lodge: _____   **Date:** _____

Funds Received *(Continued)*: _____

Lodge: _____   **Date:** _____

Debits and Checks Dispersed: _Document all outgoing payments, the amount and method of_
disbursement as well as the receiver. (Including check and transaction numbers)

Lodge: _____ **Date:** _____

Debits and Checks Dispersed: *(Continued)* _____

_____

_____

_____

_____

_____

_____

_____

_____

_____

_____

_____

_____

_____

_____

_____

_____

_____

_____

_____

_____

_____

_____

_____

_____

_____

_____

_____

_____

_____

_____

_____

_____

_____

_____

_____

_____

_____

_____

_____

_____

Lodge: _____ **Date:** _____

Debits and Checks Dispersed: *(Continued)*

Lodge: _____ **Date:** _____

Reading of the Rough Minutes: _Document finance related adjustments or corrections to the minutes._

_____
_____
_____
_____
_____
_____
_____
_____
_____
_____
_____
_____
_____
_____
_____
_____
_____
_____
_____
_____

Treasurer Report: _In this section write a summary of financial transaction that transpired in the meeting. Example: Total funds received from the Secretary and Checks Written._

Current Account Balance: _____

_____
_____
_____
_____
_____
_____
_____
_____
_____
_____
_____
_____
_____
_____
_____
_____
_____
_____

Lodge: _____ **Date:** _____

Notes: _____

_____

_____

_____

_____

_____

_____

_____

_____

_____

_____

_____

_____

_____

_____

_____

_____

_____

_____

_____

_____

_____

_____

_____

_____

_____

_____

_____

_____

_____

_____

_____

_____

_____

_____

_____

_____

_____

_____

_____

_____

_____

Lodge: _____ **Date:** _____

Notes: _____

Lodge: _____   **Date:** _____

Secretary & Treasurer Financial Reconciliation: *The Secretary and Treasurer will write a short summary*
of all funds received into the lodge by the Secretary and turned over to the Treasurer during the meeting in both books.

_____
_____
_____
_____
_____
_____
_____
_____
_____
_____
_____
_____
_____
_____
_____
_____
_____
_____
_____
_____
_____

Secretary's Signature: _____
Treasurers Signature: _____
Worshipful Masters Signature: _____

Audit Team Notes: _____
_____
_____
_____
_____
_____
_____
_____
_____
_____
_____

Audit Team Signature: _____
Audit Team Signature: _____
Audit Team Signature: _____

Lodge: _____ **Date:** _____

10th Lodge Meeting

Time of Opening: _____

Roll Call of Officers   *List the present Officer, Assistant Officer Acting Officer (with "Acting" by their name) and Visiting Brothers names.*

Worshipful Master: _____
Senior Warden: _____
Junior Warden: _____
Secretary: _____
Treasurer: _____
Senior Deacon: _____
Junior Deacon: _____
Senior Steward: _____
Junior Steward: _____
Marshal: _____
Chaplain: _____
Tyler: _____

Visiting Brothers: _____
_____
_____
_____
_____
_____
_____
_____
_____
_____
_____
_____
_____
_____
_____
_____
_____
_____
_____
_____
_____

Lodge: _____ **Date:** _____

Reading and Approval of Minutes: *Document finance related adjustments or corrections to the minutes.*

_____
_____
_____
_____
_____
_____
_____
_____
_____
_____
_____
_____
_____
_____
_____
_____
_____
_____

Treasurer Report: *In this section list the Previous Meeting Account Balance, Deposits Received, Account Debits, Current Account Balance, and Outstanding Checks.*

Current Account Balance: _____

_____
_____
_____
_____
_____
_____
_____
_____
_____
_____
_____
_____
_____
_____
_____
_____
_____

Lodge: _____ **Date:** _____

Funds Received: *In the section document all funds received from the Secretary and in what forms they were received. Example: 03 Checks: Check #'s 1123 for $100.00, 1134 for $250.00 and 2235 for $150.00, Total Checks $500.00. Total Cash Received: $250.00. Total Electronic Payments Received (verified in your service provider): $150.00. Grand Total Received: $900.00.*

_____
_____
_____
_____
_____
_____
_____
_____
_____
_____
_____
_____
_____
_____
_____
_____
_____
_____
_____
_____
_____
_____
_____
_____
_____
_____
_____
_____
_____
_____
_____
_____
_____
_____
_____
_____
_____

Lodge: _____ **Date:** _____

Funds Received *(Continued):* _____

_____

_____

_____

_____

_____

_____

_____

_____

_____

_____

_____

_____

_____

_____

_____

_____

_____

_____

_____

_____

_____

_____

_____

_____

_____

_____

_____

_____

_____

_____

_____

_____

_____

_____

_____

_____

_____

_____

Lodge: _____ **Date:** _____

Funds Received *(Continued)*: _____

_____
_____
_____
_____
_____
_____
_____
_____
_____
_____
_____
_____
_____
_____
_____
_____
_____
_____
_____
_____
_____
_____
_____
_____
_____
_____
_____
_____
_____
_____
_____
_____
_____
_____
_____
_____
_____
_____
_____
_____

Lodge: _____   **Date:** _____

Debits and Checks Dispersed: _Document all outgoing payments, the amount and method of_
disbursement as well as the receiver. (Including check and transaction numbers)

_____
_____
_____
_____
_____
_____
_____
_____
_____
_____
_____
_____
_____
_____
_____
_____
_____
_____
_____
_____
_____
_____
_____
_____
_____
_____
_____
_____
_____
_____
_____
_____
_____
_____
_____
_____
_____

Lodge: _____ **Date:** _____

Debits and Checks Dispersed: *(Continued)* _____

_____

_____

_____

_____

_____

_____

_____

_____

_____

_____

_____

_____

_____

_____

_____

_____

_____

_____

_____

_____

_____

_____

_____

_____

_____

_____

_____

_____

_____

_____

_____

_____

_____

_____

_____

_____

_____

_____

_____

_____

_____

_____

_____

_____

Lodge: _____ **Date:** _____

Debits and Checks Dispersed: *(Continued)*

_____
_____
_____
_____
_____
_____
_____
_____
_____
_____
_____
_____
_____
_____
_____
_____
_____
_____
_____
_____
_____
_____
_____
_____
_____
_____
_____
_____
_____
_____
_____
_____
_____
_____
_____
_____
_____
_____
_____
_____
_____
_____
_____

Lodge: _____   **Date:** _____

Reading of the Rough Minutes: _Document finance related adjustments or corrections to the minutes._

_____

_____

_____

_____

_____

_____

_____

_____

_____

_____

_____

_____

_____

_____

_____

_____

_____

_____

_____

Treasurer Report: _In this section write a summary of financial transaction that transpired in the meeting. Example: Total funds received from the Secretary and Checks Written._

Current Account Balance: _____

_____

_____

_____

_____

_____

_____

_____

_____

_____

_____

_____

_____

_____

_____

_____

_____

_____

_____

_____

Lodge: _____ **Date:** _____

Notes: _____

_____

_____

_____

_____

_____

_____

_____

_____

_____

_____

_____

_____

_____

_____

_____

_____

_____

_____

_____

_____

_____

_____

_____

_____

_____

_____

_____

_____

_____

_____

_____

_____

_____

_____

_____

_____

_____

_____

_____

_____

_____

Lodge: _____ **Date:** _____

Notes: _____

_____
_____
_____
_____
_____
_____
_____
_____
_____
_____
_____
_____
_____
_____
_____
_____
_____
_____
_____
_____
_____
_____
_____
_____
_____
_____
_____
_____
_____
_____
_____
_____
_____
_____
_____
_____
_____
_____
_____
_____

Lodge: _____ **Date:** _____

Secretary & Treasurer Financial Reconciliation: *The Secretary and Treasurer will write a short summary*
of all funds received into the lodge by the Secretary and turned over to the Treasurer during the meeting in both books.

_____
_____
_____
_____
_____
_____
_____
_____
_____
_____
_____
_____
_____
_____
_____
_____
_____
_____
_____

Secretary's Signature: _____
Treasurers Signature: _____
Worshipful Masters Signature: _____

Audit Team Notes: _____

_____
_____
_____
_____
_____
_____
_____
_____
_____
_____

Audit Team Signature: _____
Audit Team Signature: _____
Audit Team Signature: _____

Lodge: _____   **Date:** _____

11th Lodge Meeting

Time of Opening: _____

Roll Call of Officers   *List the present Officer, Assistant Officer Acting Officer (with "Acting" by their name) and Visiting Brothers names.*

Worshipful Master: _____
Senior Warden: _____
Junior Warden: _____
Secretary: _____
Treasurer: _____
Senior Deacon: _____
Junior Deacon: _____
Senior Steward: _____
Junior Steward: _____
Marshal: _____
Chaplain: _____
Tyler: _____

Visiting Brothers: _____
_____
_____
_____
_____
_____
_____
_____
_____
_____
_____
_____
_____
_____
_____
_____
_____
_____
_____
_____
_____

Lodge: _____ **Date:** _____

Reading and Approval of Minutes: _Document finance related adjustments or corrections to the minutes._

_____
_____
_____
_____
_____
_____
_____
_____
_____
_____
_____
_____
_____
_____
_____
_____
_____
_____

Treasurer Report: _In this section list the Previous Meeting Account Balance, Deposits Received, Account Debits, Current Account Balance, and Outstanding Checks._

Current Account Balance: _____

_____
_____
_____
_____
_____
_____
_____
_____
_____
_____
_____
_____
_____
_____
_____
_____
_____
_____

Lodge: _____   **Date:** _____

Funds Received: *In the section document all funds received from the Secretary and in what forms they were received. Example: 03 Checks: Check #'s 1123 for $100.00, 1134 for $250.00 and 2235 for $150.00, Total Checks $500.00. Total Cash Received: $250.00. Total Electronic Payments Received (verified in your service provider): $150.00. Grand Total Received: $900.00.*

Lodge: _____ **Date:** _____

Funds Received *(Continued):* _____

_____
_____
_____
_____
_____
_____
_____
_____
_____
_____
_____
_____
_____
_____
_____
_____
_____
_____
_____
_____
_____
_____
_____
_____
_____
_____
_____
_____
_____
_____
_____
_____
_____
_____
_____
_____
_____
_____
_____

Lodge: _____   **Date:** _____

Funds Received *(Continued):*   _____

_____
_____
_____
_____
_____
_____
_____
_____
_____
_____
_____
_____
_____
_____
_____
_____
_____
_____
_____
_____
_____
_____
_____
_____
_____
_____
_____
_____
_____
_____
_____
_____
_____
_____
_____
_____
_____
_____
_____

Lodge: _____ **Date:** _____

Debits and Checks Dispersed: *Document all outgoing payments, the amount and method of*
disbursement as well as the receiver. (Including check and transaction numbers)

_____
_____
_____
_____
_____
_____
_____
_____
_____
_____
_____
_____
_____
_____
_____
_____
_____
_____
_____
_____
_____
_____
_____
_____
_____
_____
_____
_____
_____
_____
_____
_____
_____
_____
_____
_____

Lodge: _____   **Date:** _____

Debits and Checks Dispersed: *(Continued)*   _____

Lodge: _____ **Date:** _____

Debits and Checks Dispersed: *(Continued)*

Lodge: _____ **Date:** _____

Reading of the Rough Minutes: *Document finance related adjustments or corrections to the minutes.*

_____
_____
_____
_____
_____
_____
_____
_____
_____
_____
_____
_____
_____
_____
_____
_____
_____
_____
_____
_____

Treasurer Report: *In this section write a summary of financial transaction that transpired in the meeting. Example: Total funds received from the Secretary and Checks Written.*

Current Account Balance: _____

_____
_____
_____
_____
_____
_____
_____
_____
_____
_____
_____
_____
_____
_____
_____
_____
_____
_____

Lodge: _____ **Date:** _____

Notes: _____

_____
_____
_____
_____
_____
_____
_____
_____
_____
_____
_____
_____
_____
_____
_____
_____
_____
_____
_____
_____
_____
_____
_____
_____
_____
_____
_____
_____
_____
_____
_____
_____
_____
_____
_____
_____
_____
_____

Lodge: _____ **Date:** _____

Notes: _____

_____
_____
_____
_____
_____
_____
_____
_____
_____
_____
_____
_____
_____
_____
_____
_____
_____
_____
_____
_____
_____
_____
_____
_____
_____
_____
_____
_____
_____
_____
_____
_____
_____
_____
_____
_____
_____
_____
_____
_____

Lodge: _____   **Date:** _____

Secretary & Treasurer Financial Reconciliation: *The Secretary and Treasurer will write a short summary*
of all funds received into the lodge by the Secretary and turned over to the Treasurer during the meeting in both books.

_____
_____
_____
_____
_____
_____
_____
_____
_____
_____
_____
_____
_____
_____
_____
_____
_____
_____
_____
_____

Secretary's Signature: _____
Treasurers Signature: _____
Worshipful Masters Signature: _____

Audit Team Notes: _____
_____
_____
_____
_____
_____
_____
_____
_____
_____

Audit Team Signature: _____
Audit Team Signature: _____
Audit Team Signature: _____

Lodge: _____   **Date:** _____

12th Lodge Meeting

Time of Opening: _____

Roll Call of Officers   *List the present Officer, Assistant Officer Acting Officer (with "Acting" by their name) and Visiting Brothers names.*

Worshipful Master: _____
Senior Warden: _____
Junior Warden: _____
Secretary: _____
Treasurer: _____
Senior Deacon: _____
Junior Deacon: _____
Senior Steward: _____
Junior Steward: _____
Marshal: _____
Chaplain: _____
Tyler: _____

Visiting Brothers: _____
_____
_____
_____
_____
_____
_____
_____
_____
_____
_____
_____
_____
_____
_____
_____
_____
_____
_____

Lodge: _____ **Date:** _____

Reading and Approval of Minutes: *Document finance related adjustments or corrections to the minutes.*

_____
_____
_____
_____
_____
_____
_____
_____
_____
_____
_____
_____
_____
_____
_____
_____
_____
_____

Treasurer Report: *In this section list the Previous Meeting Account Balance, Deposits Received, Account Debits, Current Account Balance, and Outstanding Checks.*

Current Account Balance: _____

_____
_____
_____
_____
_____
_____
_____
_____
_____
_____
_____
_____
_____
_____
_____
_____
_____
_____
_____

Lodge: _____   **Date:** _____

Funds Received: *In the section document all funds received from the Secretary and in what forms they were received. Example: 03 Checks: Check #'s 1123 for $100.00, 1134 for $250.00 and 2235 for $150.00, Total Checks $500.00. Total Cash Received: $250.00. Total Electronic Payments Received (verified in your service provider): $150.00. Grand Total Received: $900.00.*

_____
_____
_____
_____
_____
_____
_____
_____
_____
_____
_____
_____
_____
_____
_____
_____
_____
_____
_____
_____
_____
_____
_____
_____
_____
_____
_____
_____
_____
_____
_____
_____
_____
_____
_____
_____
_____
_____
_____

Lodge: _____ **Date:** _____

Funds Received *(Continued)*: _____

_____
_____
_____
_____
_____
_____
_____
_____
_____
_____
_____
_____
_____
_____
_____
_____
_____
_____
_____
_____
_____
_____
_____
_____
_____
_____
_____
_____
_____
_____
_____
_____
_____
_____
_____
_____
_____
_____
_____
_____
_____

Lodge: _____ **Date:** _____

Funds Received (*Continued*): _____

_____

_____

_____

_____

_____

_____

_____

_____

_____

_____

_____

_____

_____

_____

_____

_____

_____

_____

_____

_____

_____

_____

_____

_____

_____

_____

_____

_____

_____

_____

_____

_____

_____

_____

_____

_____

_____

_____

_____

Lodge: _____ **Date:** _____

Debits and Checks Dispersed: _Document all outgoing payments, the amount and method of_
disbursement as well as the receiver. (Including check and transaction numbers)

Lodge: _____ **Date:** _____

Debits and Checks Dispersed: *(Continued)* _____

_____

_____

_____

_____

_____

_____

_____

_____

_____

_____

_____

_____

_____

_____

_____

_____

_____

_____

_____

_____

_____

_____

_____

_____

_____

_____

_____

_____

_____

_____

_____

_____

_____

_____

_____

_____

_____

_____

_____

_____

_____

Lodge: _____   **Date:** _____

Debits and Checks Dispersed: *(Continued)*

Lodge: _____ **Date:** _____

Reading of the Rough Minutes: *Document finance related adjustments or corrections to the minutes.*

_____
_____
_____
_____
_____
_____
_____
_____
_____
_____
_____
_____
_____
_____
_____
_____
_____
_____
_____

Treasurer Report: *In this section write a summary of financial transaction that transpired in the meeting. Example: Total funds received from the Secretary and Checks Written.*

Current Account Balance: _____

_____
_____
_____
_____
_____
_____
_____
_____
_____
_____
_____
_____
_____
_____
_____
_____
_____

Lodge: _____ **Date:** _____

Notes: _____

_____
_____
_____
_____
_____
_____
_____
_____
_____
_____
_____
_____
_____
_____
_____
_____
_____
_____
_____
_____
_____
_____
_____
_____
_____
_____
_____
_____
_____
_____
_____
_____
_____
_____
_____
_____
_____
_____
_____
_____

Lodge: _____ **Date:** _____

Notes: _____

_____

_____

_____

_____

_____

_____

_____

_____

_____

_____

_____

_____

_____

_____

_____

_____

_____

_____

_____

_____

_____

_____

_____

_____

_____

_____

_____

_____

_____

_____

_____

_____

_____

_____

_____

_____

_____

_____

_____

_____

_____

_____

Lodge: _____ **Date:** _____

Secretary & Treasurer Financial Reconciliation: *The Secretary and Treasurer will write a short summary*
of all funds received into the lodge by the Secretary and turned over to the Treasurer during the meeting in both books.

_____
_____
_____
_____
_____
_____
_____
_____
_____
_____
_____
_____
_____
_____
_____
_____
_____
_____
_____
_____
_____
_____

Secretary's Signature: _____
Treasurers Signature: _____
Worshipful Masters Signature: _____

Audit Team Notes: _____
_____
_____
_____
_____
_____
_____
_____
_____
_____
_____

Audit Team Signature: _____
Audit Team Signature: _____
Audit Team Signature: _____

Lodge: _____   **Date:** _____

13th Lodge Meeting

Time of Opening: _____

Roll Call of Officers   *List the present Officer, Assistant Officer Acting Officer (with "Acting" by their name) and Visiting Brothers names.*

Worshipful Master: _____
Senior Warden: _____
Junior Warden: _____
Secretary: _____
Treasurer: _____
Senior Deacon: _____
Junior Deacon: _____
Senior Steward: _____
Junior Steward: _____
Marshal: _____
Chaplain: _____
Tyler: _____

Visiting Brothers: _____
_____
_____
_____
_____
_____
_____
_____
_____
_____
_____
_____
_____
_____
_____
_____
_____
_____
_____
_____
_____

Lodge: _____ **Date:** _____

Reading and Approval of Minutes: *Document finance related adjustments or corrections to the minutes.*

_____
_____
_____
_____
_____
_____
_____
_____
_____
_____
_____
_____
_____
_____
_____
_____
_____
_____

Treasurer Report: *In this section list the Previous Meeting Account Balance, Deposits Received, Account Debits, Current Account Balance, and Outstanding Checks.*

Current Account Balance: _____

_____
_____
_____
_____
_____
_____
_____
_____
_____
_____
_____
_____
_____
_____
_____
_____
_____
_____
_____

Lodge: _____   **Date:** _____

Funds Received: *In the section document all funds received from the Secretary and in what forms they were received. Example: 03 Checks: Check #'s 1123 for $100.00, 1134 for $250.00 and 2235 for $150.00, Total Checks $500.00. Total Cash Received: $250.00. Total Electronic Payments Received (verified in your service provider): $150.00. Grand Total Received: $900.00.*

Lodge: _____ **Date:** _____

Funds Received *(Continued)*: _____

_____
_____
_____
_____
_____
_____
_____
_____
_____
_____
_____
_____
_____
_____
_____
_____
_____
_____
_____
_____
_____
_____
_____
_____
_____
_____
_____
_____
_____
_____
_____
_____
_____
_____
_____
_____
_____
_____

Lodge: _____ **Date:** _____

Funds Received *(Continued)*: _____

_____
_____
_____
_____
_____
_____
_____
_____
_____
_____
_____
_____
_____
_____
_____
_____
_____
_____
_____
_____
_____
_____
_____
_____
_____
_____
_____
_____
_____
_____
_____
_____
_____
_____
_____
_____
_____
_____
_____

Lodge: _____   **Date:** _____

Debits and Checks Dispersed: *Document all outgoing payments, the amount and method of*
disbursement as well as the receiver. (Including check and transaction numbers)

Lodge: _____ **Date:** _____

Debits and Checks Dispersed: *(Continued)* _____

_____
_____
_____
_____
_____
_____
_____
_____
_____
_____
_____
_____
_____
_____
_____
_____
_____
_____
_____
_____
_____
_____
_____
_____
_____
_____
_____
_____
_____
_____
_____
_____
_____
_____
_____
_____
_____
_____
_____
_____
_____
_____
_____
_____
_____
_____
_____
_____
_____

Lodge: _____ **Date:** _____

Debits and Checks Dispersed: *(Continued)*

Lodge: _____   **Date:** _____

Reading of the Rough Minutes: _Document finance related adjustments or corrections to the minutes._

_____
_____
_____
_____
_____
_____
_____
_____
_____
_____
_____
_____
_____
_____
_____
_____
_____
_____

Treasurer Report: _In this section write a summary of financial transaction that transpired in the meeting. Example: Total funds received from the Secretary and Checks Written._

Current Account Balance: _____

_____
_____
_____
_____
_____
_____
_____
_____
_____
_____
_____
_____
_____
_____
_____
_____
_____
_____

Lodge: _____ **Date:** _____

Notes: _____

_____
_____
_____
_____
_____
_____
_____
_____
_____
_____
_____
_____
_____
_____
_____
_____
_____
_____
_____
_____
_____
_____
_____
_____
_____
_____
_____
_____
_____
_____
_____
_____
_____
_____
_____
_____
_____

Lodge: _____ **Date:** _____

Notes: _____

_____

_____

_____

_____

_____

_____

_____

_____

_____

_____

_____

_____

_____

_____

_____

_____

_____

_____

_____

_____

_____

_____

_____

_____

_____

_____

_____

_____

_____

_____

_____

_____

_____

_____

_____

_____

_____

_____

_____

_____

_____

_____

_____

_____

Lodge: _____ **Date:** _____

Secretary & Treasurer Financial Reconciliation: *The Secretary and Treasurer will write a short summary*
of all funds received into the lodge by the Secretary and turned over to the Treasurer during the meeting in both books.

_____
_____
_____
_____
_____
_____
_____
_____
_____
_____
_____
_____
_____
_____
_____
_____
_____
_____
_____
_____

Secretary's Signature: _____
Treasurers Signature: _____
Worshipful Masters Signature: _____

Audit Team Notes: _____
_____
_____
_____
_____
_____
_____
_____
_____
_____
_____

Audit Team Signature: _____
Audit Team Signature: _____
Audit Team Signature: _____

Lodge: _____   **Date:** _____

14th Lodge Meeting

Time of Opening: _____

Roll Call of Officers

List the present Officer, Assistant Officer Acting Officer (with "Acting" by their name) and Visiting Brothers names.

Worshipful Master: _____

Senior Warden: _____

Junior Warden: _____

Secretary: _____

Treasurer: _____

Senior Deacon: _____

Junior Deacon: _____

Senior Steward: _____

Junior Steward: _____

Marshal: _____

Chaplain: _____

Tyler: _____

Visiting Brothers: _____

_____

_____

_____

_____

_____

_____

_____

_____

_____

_____

_____

_____

_____

_____

_____

_____

_____

_____

_____

Lodge: _____   **Date:** _____

Reading and Approval of Minutes: *Document finance related adjustments or corrections to the minutes.*

_____

_____

_____

_____

_____

_____

_____

_____

_____

_____

_____

_____

_____

_____

_____

_____

_____

Treasurer Report: *In this section list the Previous Meeting Account Balance, Deposits Received, Account Debits, Current Account Balance, and Outstanding Checks.*

Current Account Balance: _____

_____

_____

_____

_____

_____

_____

_____

_____

_____

_____

_____

_____

_____

_____

_____

_____

_____

_____

Lodge: _____ **Date:** _____

Funds Received: *In the section document all funds received from the Secretary and in what forms they were received. Example: 03 Checks: Check #'s 1123 for $100.00, 1134 for $250.00 and 2235 for $150.00, Total Checks $500.00. Total Cash Received: $250.00. Total Electronic Payments Received (verified in your service provider): $150.00. Grand Total Received: $900.00.*

_____

_____

_____

_____

_____

_____

_____

_____

_____

_____

_____

_____

_____

_____

_____

_____

_____

_____

_____

_____

_____

_____

_____

_____

_____

_____

_____

_____

_____

_____

_____

_____

_____

_____

_____

_____

_____

_____

_____

Lodge: _____ **Date:** _____

Funds Received *(Continued)*: _____

_____
_____
_____
_____
_____
_____
_____
_____
_____
_____
_____
_____
_____
_____
_____
_____
_____
_____
_____
_____
_____
_____
_____
_____
_____
_____
_____
_____
_____
_____
_____
_____
_____
_____
_____
_____
_____
_____
_____
_____
_____

Lodge: _____ **Date:** _____

Funds Received *(Continued)*: _____

_____
_____
_____
_____
_____
_____
_____
_____
_____
_____
_____
_____
_____
_____
_____
_____
_____
_____
_____
_____
_____
_____
_____
_____
_____
_____
_____
_____
_____
_____
_____
_____
_____
_____
_____
_____
_____
_____
_____
_____
_____

Lodge: _____   **Date:** _____

Debits and Checks Dispersed: *Document all outgoing payments, the amount and method of*
disbursement as well as the receiver. (Including check and transaction numbers)

_____
_____
_____
_____
_____
_____
_____
_____
_____
_____
_____
_____
_____
_____
_____
_____
_____
_____
_____
_____
_____
_____
_____
_____
_____
_____
_____
_____
_____
_____
_____
_____
_____
_____
_____
_____
_____
_____

Lodge: _____ **Date:** _____

Debits and Checks Dispersed: *(Continued)* _____

Lodge: _____ **Date:** _____

Debits and Checks Dispersed: *(Continued)*

Lodge: _____   **Date:** _____

Reading of the Rough Minutes: *Document finance related adjustments or corrections to the minutes.*

_____
_____
_____
_____
_____
_____
_____
_____
_____
_____
_____
_____
_____
_____
_____
_____
_____
_____
_____

Treasurer Report: *In this section write a summary of financial transaction that transpired in the meeting. Example: Total funds received from the Secretary and Checks Written.*

Current Account Balance: _____

_____
_____
_____
_____
_____
_____
_____
_____
_____
_____
_____
_____
_____
_____
_____
_____
_____
_____

Lodge: _____   **Date:** _____

Notes: _____

_____

_____

_____

_____

_____

_____

_____

_____

_____

_____

_____

_____

_____

_____

_____

_____

_____

_____

_____

_____

_____

_____

_____

_____

_____

_____

_____

_____

_____

_____

_____

_____

_____

_____

_____

_____

_____

_____

_____

_____

Lodge: _____ **Date:** _____

Notes: _____

_____

_____

_____

_____

_____

_____

_____

_____

_____

_____

_____

_____

_____

_____

_____

_____

_____

_____

_____

_____

_____

_____

_____

_____

_____

_____

_____

_____

_____

_____

_____

_____

_____

_____

_____

_____

_____

_____

Lodge: _____ **Date:** _____

Secretary & Treasurer Financial Reconciliation: *The Secretary and Treasurer will write a short summary*
of all funds received into the lodge by the Secretary and turned over to the Treasurer during the meeting in both books.

_____
_____
_____
_____
_____
_____
_____
_____
_____
_____
_____
_____
_____
_____
_____
_____
_____
_____
_____
_____
_____

Secretary's Signature: _____
Treasurers Signature: _____
Worshipful Masters Signature: _____

Audit Team Notes: _____
_____
_____
_____
_____
_____
_____
_____
_____
_____

Audit Team Signature: _____
Audit Team Signature: _____
Audit Team Signature: _____

Lodge: _____   **Date:** _____

15th **Lodge Meeting**

Time of Opening: _____

Roll Call of Officers   *List the present Officer, Assistant Officer Acting Officer (with "Acting" by their name) and Visiting Brothers names.*

Worshipful Master: _____
Senior Warden: _____
Junior Warden: _____
Secretary: _____
Treasurer: _____
Senior Deacon: _____
Junior Deacon: _____
Senior Steward: _____
Junior Steward: _____
Marshal: _____
Chaplain: _____
Tyler: _____

Visiting Brothers: _____
_____
_____
_____
_____
_____
_____
_____
_____
_____
_____
_____
_____
_____
_____
_____
_____
_____
_____
_____

Lodge: _____ **Date:** _____

Reading and Approval of Minutes: *Document finance related adjustments or corrections to the minutes.*

_____
_____
_____
_____
_____
_____
_____
_____
_____
_____
_____
_____
_____
_____
_____
_____
_____
_____

Treasurer Report: *In this section list the Previous Meeting Account Balance, Deposits Received, Account Debits, Current Account Balance, and Outstanding Checks.*

Current Account Balance: _____

_____
_____
_____
_____
_____
_____
_____
_____
_____
_____
_____
_____
_____
_____
_____
_____
_____
_____

Lodge: _____   **Date:** _____

Funds Received: *In the section document all funds received from the Secretary and in what forms they were received. Example: 03 Checks: Check #'s 1123 for $100.00, 1134 for $250.00 and 2235 for $150.00, Total Checks $500.00. Total Cash Received: $250.00. Total Electronic Payments Received (verified in your service provider): $150.00. Grand Total Received: $900.00.*

_____
_____
_____
_____
_____
_____
_____
_____
_____
_____
_____
_____
_____
_____
_____
_____
_____
_____
_____
_____
_____
_____
_____
_____
_____
_____
_____
_____
_____
_____
_____
_____
_____
_____
_____
_____

Lodge: _____ **Date:** _____

Funds Received (*Continued*): _____

_____
_____
_____
_____
_____
_____
_____
_____
_____
_____
_____
_____
_____
_____
_____
_____
_____
_____
_____
_____
_____
_____
_____
_____
_____
_____
_____
_____
_____
_____
_____
_____
_____
_____
_____
_____
_____
_____
_____

Lodge: _____ **Date:** _____

Funds Received *(Continued)*: _____

_____

_____

_____

_____

_____

_____

_____

_____

_____

_____

_____

_____

_____

_____

_____

_____

_____

_____

_____

_____

_____

_____

_____

_____

_____

_____

_____

_____

_____

_____

_____

_____

_____

_____

_____

_____

_____

_____

_____

_____

Lodge: _____ **Date:** _____

Debits and Checks Dispersed: *Document all outgoing payments, the amount and method of disbursement as well as the receiver. (Including check and transaction numbers)*

_____
_____
_____
_____
_____
_____
_____
_____
_____
_____
_____
_____
_____
_____
_____
_____
_____
_____
_____
_____
_____
_____
_____
_____
_____
_____
_____
_____
_____
_____
_____
_____
_____
_____
_____
_____
_____
_____
_____

Lodge: _____ **Date:** _____

Debits and Checks Dispersed: *(Continued)* _____

_____

_____

_____

_____

_____

_____

_____

_____

_____

_____

_____

_____

_____

_____

_____

_____

_____

_____

_____

_____

_____

_____

_____

_____

_____

_____

_____

_____

_____

_____

_____

_____

_____

_____

_____

_____

_____

_____

_____

_____

_____

Lodge: _____ **Date:** _____

Debits and Checks Dispersed: *(Continued)*

_____
_____
_____
_____
_____
_____
_____
_____
_____
_____
_____
_____
_____
_____
_____
_____
_____
_____
_____
_____
_____
_____
_____
_____
_____
_____
_____
_____
_____
_____
_____
_____
_____
_____
_____
_____
_____
_____
_____
_____
_____
_____
_____
_____

Lodge: _____ **Date:** _____

Reading of the Rough Minutes: *Document finance related adjustments or corrections to the minutes.*

_____
_____
_____
_____
_____
_____
_____
_____
_____
_____
_____
_____
_____
_____
_____
_____
_____
_____
_____
_____

Treasurer Report: *In this section write a summary of financial transaction that transpired in the meeting. Example: Total funds received from the Secretary and Checks Written.*

Current Account Balance: _____

_____
_____
_____
_____
_____
_____
_____
_____
_____
_____
_____
_____
_____
_____
_____
_____
_____
_____
_____

Lodge: _____ **Date:** _____

Notes: _____

_____
_____
_____
_____
_____
_____
_____
_____
_____
_____
_____
_____
_____
_____
_____
_____
_____
_____
_____
_____
_____
_____
_____
_____
_____
_____
_____
_____
_____
_____
_____
_____
_____
_____
_____
_____
_____
_____
_____
_____

Lodge: _____   **Date:** _____

Notes: _____

_____
_____
_____
_____
_____
_____
_____
_____
_____
_____
_____
_____
_____
_____
_____
_____
_____
_____
_____
_____
_____
_____
_____
_____
_____
_____
_____
_____
_____
_____
_____
_____
_____
_____
_____
_____
_____
_____
_____
_____
_____
_____
_____
_____
_____
_____
_____

Lodge: _____ **Date:** _____

Secretary & Treasurer Financial Reconciliation: *The Secretary and Treasurer will write a short summary*
of all funds received into the lodge by the Secretary and turned over to the Treasurer during the meeting in both books.

_____
_____
_____
_____
_____
_____
_____
_____
_____
_____
_____
_____
_____
_____
_____
_____
_____
_____
_____
_____

Secretary's Signature: _____
Treasurers Signature: _____
Worshipful Masters Signature: _____

Audit Team Notes: _____

_____
_____
_____
_____
_____
_____
_____
_____
_____
_____

Audit Team Signature: _____
Audit Team Signature: _____
Audit Team Signature: _____

Lodge: _____   **Date:** _____

16th Lodge Meeting

Time of Opening: _____

Roll Call of Officers   *List the present Officer, Assistant Officer Acting Officer (with "Acting" by their name) and Visiting Brothers names.*

Worshipful Master: _____
Senior Warden: _____
Junior Warden: _____
Secretary: _____
Treasurer: _____
Senior Deacon: _____
Junior Deacon: _____
Senior Steward: _____
Junior Steward: _____
Marshal: _____
Chaplain: _____
Tyler: _____

Visiting Brothers: _____
_____
_____
_____
_____
_____
_____
_____
_____
_____
_____
_____
_____
_____
_____
_____
_____
_____
_____

Lodge: _____ **Date:** _____

Reading and Approval of Minutes: *Document finance related adjustments or corrections to the minutes.*

_____
_____
_____
_____
_____
_____
_____
_____
_____
_____
_____
_____
_____
_____
_____
_____
_____
_____

Treasurer Report: *In this section list the Previous Meeting Account Balance, Deposits Received, Account Debits, Current Account Balance, and Outstanding Checks.*

Current Account Balance: _____

_____
_____
_____
_____
_____
_____
_____
_____
_____
_____
_____
_____
_____
_____
_____
_____
_____
_____
_____
_____

Lodge: _____   **Date:** _____

Funds Received: *In the section document all funds received from the Secretary and in what forms they were received. Example: 03 Checks: Check #'s 1123 for $100.00, 1134 for $250.00 and 2235 for $150.00, Total Checks $500.00. Total Cash Received: $250.00. Total Electronic Payments Received (verified in your service provider): $150.00. Grand Total Received: $900.00.*

_____
_____
_____
_____
_____
_____
_____
_____
_____
_____
_____
_____
_____
_____
_____
_____
_____
_____
_____
_____
_____
_____
_____
_____
_____
_____
_____
_____
_____
_____
_____
_____
_____
_____
_____

Lodge: _____ **Date:** _____

Funds Received *(Continued)*: _____

_____

_____

_____

_____

_____

_____

_____

_____

_____

_____

_____

_____

_____

_____

_____

_____

_____

_____

_____

_____

_____

_____

_____

_____

_____

_____

_____

_____

_____

_____

_____

_____

_____

_____

_____

_____

_____

_____

_____

_____

_____

_____

_____

_____

Lodge: _____ **Date:** _____

Funds Received *(Continued)*: _____

_____
_____
_____
_____
_____
_____
_____
_____
_____
_____
_____
_____
_____
_____
_____
_____
_____
_____
_____
_____
_____
_____
_____
_____
_____
_____
_____
_____
_____
_____
_____
_____
_____
_____
_____
_____
_____
_____

Lodge: _____   **Date:** _____

Debits and Checks Dispersed: _Document all outgoing payments, the amount and method of_
disbursement as well as the receiver. (Including check and transaction numbers)

Lodge: _____ **Date:** _____

Debits and Checks Dispersed: *(Continued)* _____

_____

_____

_____

_____

_____

_____

_____

_____

_____

_____

_____

_____

_____

_____

_____

_____

_____

_____

_____

_____

_____

_____

_____

_____

_____

_____

_____

_____

_____

_____

_____

_____

_____

_____

_____

_____

_____

_____

_____

_____

_____

_____

_____

_____

Lodge: _____ **Date:** _____

Debits and Checks Dispersed: *(Continued)*

Lodge: _____ **Date:** _____

Reading of the Rough Minutes: *Document finance related adjustments or corrections to the minutes.*

_____
_____
_____
_____
_____
_____
_____
_____
_____
_____
_____
_____
_____
_____
_____
_____
_____
_____
_____

Treasurer Report: *In this section write a summary of financial transaction that transpired in the meeting. Example: Total funds received from the Secretary and Checks Written.*

Current Account Balance: _____

_____
_____
_____
_____
_____
_____
_____
_____
_____
_____
_____
_____
_____
_____
_____
_____
_____
_____
_____

Lodge: _____   **Date:** _____

Notes: _____

_____
_____
_____
_____
_____
_____
_____
_____
_____
_____
_____
_____
_____
_____
_____
_____
_____
_____
_____
_____
_____
_____
_____
_____
_____
_____
_____
_____
_____
_____
_____
_____
_____
_____
_____
_____

Lodge: _____   **Date:** _____

Notes: _____

_____
_____
_____
_____
_____
_____
_____
_____
_____
_____
_____
_____
_____
_____
_____
_____
_____
_____
_____
_____
_____
_____
_____
_____
_____
_____
_____
_____
_____
_____
_____
_____
_____
_____
_____
_____
_____
_____
_____
_____
_____
_____
_____
_____

Lodge: _____ **Date:** _____

Secretary & Treasurer Financial Reconciliation: *The Secretary and Treasurer will write a short summary*
of all funds received into the lodge by the Secretary and turned over to the Treasurer during the meeting in both books.

_____
_____
_____
_____
_____
_____
_____
_____
_____
_____
_____
_____
_____
_____
_____
_____
_____
_____
_____
_____
_____
_____

Secretary's Signature: _____
Treasurers Signature: _____
Worshipful Masters Signature: _____

Audit Team Notes: _____
_____
_____
_____
_____
_____
_____
_____
_____
_____
_____

Audit Team Signature: _____
Audit Team Signature: _____
Audit Team Signature: _____

Lodge: _____   **Date:** _____

17th Lodge Meeting

Time of Opening: _____

Roll Call of Officers   *List the present Officer, Assistant Officer Acting Officer (with "Acting" by their name) and Visiting Brothers names.*

Worshipful Master: _____
Senior Warden: _____
Junior Warden: _____
Secretary: _____
Treasurer: _____
Senior Deacon: _____
Junior Deacon: _____
Senior Steward: _____
Junior Steward: _____
Marshal: _____
Chaplain: _____
Tyler: _____

Visiting Brothers: _____

_____
_____
_____
_____
_____
_____
_____
_____
_____
_____
_____
_____
_____
_____
_____
_____
_____
_____

Lodge: _____   **Date:** _____

Reading and Approval of Minutes: *Document finance related adjustments or corrections to the minutes.*

_____
_____
_____
_____
_____
_____
_____
_____
_____
_____
_____
_____
_____
_____
_____
_____

Treasurer Report: *In this section list the Previous Meeting Account Balance, Deposits Received, Account Debits, Current Account Balance, and Outstanding Checks.*

Current Account Balance: _____

_____
_____
_____
_____
_____
_____
_____
_____
_____
_____
_____
_____
_____
_____
_____
_____
_____
_____

Lodge: _____ **Date:** _____

Funds Received: *In the section document all funds received from the Secretary and in what forms they were received. Example: 03 Checks: Check #'s 1123 for $100.00, 1134 for $250.00 and 2235 for $150.00, Total Checks $500.00. Total Cash Received: $250.00. Total Electronic Payments Received (verified in your service provider): $150.00. Grand Total Received: $900.00.*

Lodge: _____   **Date:** _____

Funds Received *(Continued):*   _____

_____
_____
_____
_____
_____
_____
_____
_____
_____
_____
_____
_____
_____
_____
_____
_____
_____
_____
_____
_____
_____
_____
_____
_____
_____
_____
_____
_____
_____
_____
_____
_____
_____
_____
_____
_____
_____
_____
_____
_____

Lodge: _____ **Date:** _____

Funds Received *(Continued):* _____

_____
_____
_____
_____
_____
_____
_____
_____
_____
_____
_____
_____
_____
_____
_____
_____
_____
_____
_____
_____
_____
_____
_____
_____
_____
_____
_____
_____
_____
_____
_____
_____
_____
_____
_____
_____
_____
_____
_____

Lodge: _____ **Date:** _____

Debits and Checks Dispersed: _Document all outgoing payments, the amount and method of disbursement as well as the receiver. (Including check and transaction numbers)_

Lodge: _____   **Date:** _____

Debits and Checks Dispersed: *(Continued)* _____

_____
_____
_____
_____
_____
_____
_____
_____
_____
_____
_____
_____
_____
_____
_____
_____
_____
_____
_____
_____
_____
_____
_____
_____
_____
_____
_____
_____
_____
_____
_____
_____
_____
_____
_____
_____
_____
_____
_____
_____
_____
_____
_____
_____

Lodge: _____ **Date:** _____

Debits and Checks Dispersed: *(Continued)*

Lodge: _____   **Date:** _____

Reading of the Rough Minutes: *Document finance related adjustments or corrections to the minutes.*

_____
_____
_____
_____
_____
_____
_____
_____
_____
_____
_____
_____
_____
_____
_____
_____
_____
_____

Treasurer Report: *In this section write a summary of financial transaction that transpired in the meeting. Example: Total funds received from the Secretary and Checks Written.*

Current Account Balance: _____

_____
_____
_____
_____
_____
_____
_____
_____
_____
_____
_____
_____
_____
_____
_____
_____
_____

Lodge: _____   **Date:** _____

Notes: _____

_____

_____

_____

_____

_____

_____

_____

_____

_____

_____

_____

_____

_____

_____

_____

_____

_____

_____

_____

_____

_____

_____

_____

_____

_____

_____

_____

_____

_____

_____

_____

_____

_____

_____

_____

_____

Lodge: _____ **Date:** _____

Notes:

_____

_____

_____

_____

_____

_____

_____

_____

_____

_____

_____

_____

_____

_____

_____

_____

_____

_____

_____

_____

_____

_____

_____

_____

_____

_____

_____

_____

_____

_____

_____

_____

_____

_____

_____

_____

_____

_____

_____

_____

_____

_____

Lodge: _____ **Date:** _____

Secretary & Treasurer Financial Reconciliation: *The Secretary and Treasurer will write a short summary of all funds received into the lodge by the Secretary and turned over to the Treasurer during the meeting in both books.*

_____
_____
_____
_____
_____
_____
_____
_____
_____
_____
_____
_____
_____
_____
_____
_____
_____
_____
_____
_____
_____
_____

Secretary's Signature: _____
Treasurers Signature: _____
Worshipful Masters Signature: _____

Audit Team Notes: _____
_____
_____
_____
_____
_____
_____
_____
_____
_____
_____

Audit Team Signature: _____
Audit Team Signature: _____
Audit Team Signature: _____

Lodge: _____   **Date:** _____

18th Lodge Meeting

Time of Opening: _____

Roll Call of Officers   *List the present Officer, Assistant Officer Acting Officer (with "Acting" by their name) and Visiting Brothers names.*

Worshipful Master: _____
Senior Warden: _____
Junior Warden: _____
Secretary: _____
Treasurer: _____
Senior Deacon: _____
Junior Deacon: _____
Senior Steward: _____
Junior Steward: _____
Marshal: _____
Chaplain: _____
Tyler: _____

Visiting Brothers: _____

_____
_____
_____
_____
_____
_____
_____
_____
_____
_____
_____
_____
_____
_____
_____
_____
_____
_____
_____

Lodge: _____   **Date:** _____

Reading and Approval of Minutes: *Document finance related adjustments or corrections to the minutes.*

_____
_____
_____
_____
_____
_____
_____
_____
_____
_____
_____
_____
_____
_____
_____
_____
_____

Treasurer Report: *In this section list the Previous Meeting Account Balance, Deposits Received, Account Debits, Current Account Balance, and Outstanding Checks.*

Current Account Balance: _____

_____
_____
_____
_____
_____
_____
_____
_____
_____
_____
_____
_____
_____
_____
_____
_____
_____
_____

Lodge: _____   **Date:** _____

Funds Received: *In the section document all funds received from the Secretary and in what forms they were received. Example: 03 Checks: Check #'s 1123 for $100.00, 1134 for $250.00 and 2235 for $150.00, Total Checks $500.00. Total Cash Received: $250.00. Total Electronic Payments Received (verified in your service provider): $150.00. Grand Total Received: $900.00.*

_____
_____
_____
_____
_____
_____
_____
_____
_____
_____
_____
_____
_____
_____
_____
_____
_____
_____
_____
_____
_____
_____
_____
_____
_____
_____
_____
_____
_____
_____
_____
_____
_____
_____

Lodge: _____ **Date:** _____

Funds Received *(Continued)*: _____

_____
_____
_____
_____
_____
_____
_____
_____
_____
_____
_____
_____
_____
_____
_____
_____
_____
_____
_____
_____
_____
_____
_____
_____
_____
_____
_____
_____
_____
_____
_____
_____
_____
_____
_____
_____
_____
_____

Lodge: _____ **Date:** _____

Funds Received *(Continued)*: _____

_____

_____

_____

_____

_____

_____

_____

_____

_____

_____

_____

_____

_____

_____

_____

_____

_____

_____

_____

_____

_____

_____

_____

_____

_____

_____

_____

_____

_____

_____

_____

_____

_____

_____

_____

_____

_____

_____

_____

_____

_____

_____

_____

_____

Lodge: _____   **Date:** _____

Debits and Checks Dispersed: *Document all outgoing payments, the amount and method of*
disbursement as well as the receiver. (Including check and transaction numbers)

_____
_____
_____
_____
_____
_____
_____
_____
_____
_____
_____
_____
_____
_____
_____
_____
_____
_____
_____
_____
_____
_____
_____
_____
_____
_____
_____
_____
_____
_____
_____
_____
_____
_____
_____
_____
_____
_____
_____
_____
_____
_____
_____

Lodge: _____ **Date:** _____

Debits and Checks Dispersed: *(Continued)* _____

Lodge: _____ **Date:** _____

Debits and Checks Dispersed: *(Continued)*

_____
_____
_____
_____
_____
_____
_____
_____
_____
_____
_____
_____
_____
_____
_____
_____
_____
_____
_____
_____
_____
_____
_____
_____
_____
_____
_____
_____
_____
_____
_____
_____
_____
_____
_____
_____
_____
_____
_____
_____

Lodge: _____ **Date:** _____

Reading of the Rough Minutes: *Document finance related adjustments or corrections to the minutes.*

_____
_____
_____
_____
_____
_____
_____
_____
_____
_____
_____
_____
_____
_____
_____
_____
_____
_____
_____

Treasurer Report: *In this section write a summary of financial transaction that transpired in the meeting. Example: Total funds received from the Secretary and Checks Written.*

Current Account Balance: _____

_____
_____
_____
_____
_____
_____
_____
_____
_____
_____
_____
_____
_____
_____
_____
_____
_____

Lodge: _____ **Date:** _____

Notes: _____

_____
_____
_____
_____
_____
_____
_____
_____
_____
_____
_____
_____
_____
_____
_____
_____
_____
_____
_____
_____
_____
_____
_____
_____
_____
_____
_____
_____
_____
_____
_____
_____
_____
_____
_____
_____
_____
_____
_____
_____

Lodge: _____ **Date:** _____

Notes: _____

_____
_____
_____
_____
_____
_____
_____
_____
_____
_____
_____
_____
_____
_____
_____
_____
_____
_____
_____
_____
_____
_____
_____
_____
_____
_____
_____
_____
_____
_____
_____
_____
_____
_____
_____
_____
_____
_____
_____
_____
_____
_____
_____

Lodge: _____   **Date:** _____

Secretary & Treasurer Financial Reconciliation: *The Secretary and Treasurer will write a short summary*
of all funds received into the lodge by the Secretary and turned over to the Treasurer during the meeting in both books.

_____
_____
_____
_____
_____
_____
_____
_____
_____
_____
_____
_____
_____
_____
_____
_____
_____
_____
_____

Secretary's Signature: _____
Treasurers Signature: _____
Worshipful Masters Signature: _____

Audit Team Notes: _____
_____
_____
_____
_____
_____
_____
_____
_____
_____
_____

Audit Team Signature: _____
Audit Team Signature: _____
Audit Team Signature: _____

Lodge: _____   **Date:** _____

19th **Lodge Meeting**

Time of Opening: _____

Roll Call of Officers   *List the present Officer, Assistant Officer Acting Officer (with "Acting" by their name) and Visiting Brothers names.*

Worshipful Master: _____

Senior Warden: _____

Junior Warden: _____

Secretary: _____

Treasurer: _____

Senior Deacon: _____

Junior Deacon: _____

Senior Steward: _____

Junior Steward: _____

Marshal: _____

Chaplain: _____

Tyler: _____

Visiting Brothers: _____

_____

_____

_____

_____

_____

_____

_____

_____

_____

_____

_____

_____

_____

_____

_____

_____

_____

_____

_____

_____

Lodge: _____   **Date:** _____ , _____

Reading and Approval of Minutes: _Document finance related adjustments or corrections to the minutes._

_____
_____
_____
_____
_____
_____
_____
_____
_____
_____
_____
_____
_____
_____
_____
_____

Treasurer Report: _In this section list the Previous Meeting Account Balance, Deposits Received, Account Debits, Current Account Balance, and Outstanding Checks._

Current Account Balance: _____

_____
_____
_____
_____
_____
_____
_____
_____
_____
_____
_____
_____
_____
_____
_____
_____
_____

Lodge: _____ **Date:** _____

Funds Received: _In the section document all funds received from the Secretary and in what forms they were received. Example: 03 Checks: Check #'s 1123 for $100.00, 1134 for $250.00 and 2235 for $150.00, Total Checks $500.00. Total Cash Received: $250.00. Total Electronic Payments Received (verified in your service provider): $150.00. Grand Total Received: $900.00._

_____
_____
_____
_____
_____
_____
_____
_____
_____
_____
_____
_____
_____
_____
_____
_____
_____
_____
_____
_____
_____
_____
_____
_____
_____
_____
_____
_____
_____
_____
_____
_____
_____
_____
_____
_____

Lodge: _____   **Date:** _____

Funds Received (*Continued*):   _____

_____
_____
_____
_____
_____
_____
_____
_____
_____
_____
_____
_____
_____
_____
_____
_____
_____
_____
_____
_____
_____
_____
_____
_____
_____
_____
_____
_____
_____
_____
_____
_____
_____
_____
_____
_____
_____
_____
_____
_____

Lodge: _____ **Date:** _____

Funds Received *(Continued):* _____

_____
_____
_____
_____
_____
_____
_____
_____
_____
_____
_____
_____
_____
_____
_____
_____
_____
_____
_____
_____
_____
_____
_____
_____
_____
_____
_____
_____
_____
_____
_____
_____
_____
_____
_____
_____
_____
_____
_____
_____
_____
_____
_____
_____
_____
_____
_____

Lodge: _____ **Date:** _____

Debits and Checks Dispersed: *Document all outgoing payments, the amount and method of disbursement as well as the receiver. (Including check and transaction numbers)*

_____
_____
_____
_____
_____
_____
_____
_____
_____
_____
_____
_____
_____
_____
_____
_____
_____
_____
_____
_____
_____
_____
_____
_____
_____
_____
_____
_____
_____
_____
_____
_____
_____
_____

Lodge: _____ **Date:** _____

Debits and Checks Dispersed: *(Continued)* _____

_____
_____
_____
_____
_____
_____
_____
_____
_____
_____
_____
_____
_____
_____
_____
_____
_____
_____
_____
_____
_____
_____
_____
_____
_____
_____
_____
_____
_____
_____
_____
_____
_____
_____
_____
_____
_____
_____
_____
_____
_____
_____
_____
_____
_____
_____
_____

Lodge: _____ **Date:** _____

Debits and Checks Dispersed: *(Continued)*

Lodge: _____   **Date:** _____

Reading of the Rough Minutes: *Document finance related adjustments or corrections to the minutes.*

_____
_____
_____
_____
_____
_____
_____
_____
_____
_____
_____
_____
_____
_____
_____
_____
_____
_____

Treasurer Report: *In this section write a summary of financial transaction that transpired in the meeting. Example: Total funds received from the Secretary and Checks Written.*

Current Account Balance: _____

_____
_____
_____
_____
_____
_____
_____
_____
_____
_____
_____
_____
_____
_____
_____
_____
_____

Lodge: _____ **Date:** _____

Notes: _____

_____

_____

_____

_____

_____

_____

_____

_____

_____

_____

_____

_____

_____

_____

_____

_____

_____

_____

_____

_____

_____

_____

_____

_____

_____

_____

_____

_____

_____

_____

_____

_____

_____

_____

_____

_____

_____

_____

_____

Lodge: _____ **Date:** _____

Notes: _____

_____
_____
_____
_____
_____
_____
_____
_____
_____
_____
_____
_____
_____
_____
_____
_____
_____
_____
_____
_____
_____
_____
_____
_____
_____
_____
_____
_____
_____
_____
_____
_____
_____
_____
_____
_____
_____
_____
_____
_____

Lodge: _____ **Date:** _____

Secretary & Treasurer Financial Reconciliation: *The Secretary and Treasurer will write a short summary*
of all funds received into the lodge by the Secretary and turned over to the Treasurer during the meeting in both books.

_____
_____
_____
_____
_____
_____
_____
_____
_____
_____
_____
_____
_____
_____
_____
_____
_____
_____
_____
_____
_____

Secretary's Signature: _____
Treasurers Signature: _____
Worshipful Masters Signature: _____

Audit Team Notes: _____

_____
_____
_____
_____
_____
_____
_____
_____
_____

Audit Team Signature: _____
Audit Team Signature: _____
Audit Team Signature: _____

Lodge: _____   **Date:** _____

20th Lodge Meeting

Time of Opening: _____

Roll Call of Officers   *List the present Officer, Assistant Officer Acting Officer (with "Acting" by their*
                             name) and Visiting Brothers names.

Worshipful Master: _____
Senior Warden: _____
Junior Warden: _____
Secretary: _____
Treasurer: _____
Senior Deacon: _____
Junior Deacon: _____
Senior Steward: _____
Junior Steward: _____
Marshal: _____
Chaplain: _____
Tyler: _____

Visiting Brothers: _____
                      _____
                      _____
                      _____
                      _____
                      _____
                      _____
                      _____
                      _____
                      _____
                      _____
                      _____
                      _____
                      _____
                      _____
                      _____
                      _____
                      _____
                      _____
                      _____

Lodge: _____ **Date:** _____

Reading and Approval of Minutes: *Document finance related adjustments or corrections to the minutes.*

_____
_____
_____
_____
_____
_____
_____
_____
_____
_____
_____
_____
_____
_____
_____
_____

Treasurer Report: *In this section list the Previous Meeting Account Balance, Deposits Received, Account Debits, Current Account Balance, and Outstanding Checks.*

Current Account Balance: _____

_____
_____
_____
_____
_____
_____
_____
_____
_____
_____
_____
_____
_____
_____
_____
_____
_____
_____

Lodge: _____   **Date:** _____

Funds Received: _In the section document all funds received from the Secretary and in what forms they_
were received. Example: 03 Checks: Check #'s 1123 for $100.00, 1134 for $250.00 and 2235 for $150.00, Total
Checks $500.00. Total Cash Received: $250.00. Total Electronic Payments Received (verified in your service
provider): $150.00. Grand Total Received: $900.00.

Lodge: _____ **Date:** _____

Funds Received *(Continued)*: _____

_____
_____
_____
_____
_____
_____
_____
_____
_____
_____
_____
_____
_____
_____
_____
_____
_____
_____
_____
_____
_____
_____
_____
_____
_____
_____
_____
_____
_____
_____
_____
_____
_____
_____
_____
_____
_____
_____
_____
_____
_____
_____

Lodge: _____ **Date:** _____

Funds Received *(Continued)*:   _____

_____

_____

_____

_____

_____

_____

_____

_____

_____

_____

_____

_____

_____

_____

_____

_____

_____

_____

_____

_____

_____

_____

_____

_____

_____

_____

_____

_____

_____

_____

_____

_____

_____

_____

_____

_____

_____

_____

_____

Lodge: _____   **Date:** _____

Debits and Checks Dispersed: *Document all outgoing payments, the amount and method of*
disbursement as well as the receiver. (Including check and transaction numbers)

Lodge: _____ **Date:** _____

Debits and Checks Dispersed: *(Continued)* _____

_____
_____
_____
_____
_____
_____
_____
_____
_____
_____
_____
_____
_____
_____
_____
_____
_____
_____
_____
_____
_____
_____
_____
_____
_____
_____
_____
_____
_____
_____
_____
_____
_____
_____
_____
_____
_____
_____
_____
_____
_____

Lodge: _____ **Date:** _____

Debits and Checks Dispersed: *(Continued)*

Debits and Checks Dispersed: *(Continued)*

Lodge: _____ **Date:** _____

Reading of the Rough Minutes: _Document finance related adjustments or corrections to the minutes._

_____
_____
_____
_____
_____
_____
_____
_____
_____
_____
_____
_____
_____
_____
_____
_____
_____
_____
_____

Treasurer Report: _In this section write a summary of financial transaction that transpired in the meeting. Example: Total funds received from the Secretary and Checks Written._

Current Account Balance: _____

_____
_____
_____
_____
_____
_____
_____
_____
_____
_____
_____
_____
_____
_____
_____
_____
_____

Lodge: _____ **Date:** _____

Notes: _____

_____

Lodge: _____   **Date:** _____

Notes: _____

_____
_____
_____
_____
_____
_____
_____
_____
_____
_____
_____
_____
_____
_____
_____
_____
_____
_____
_____
_____
_____
_____
_____
_____
_____
_____
_____
_____
_____
_____
_____
_____
_____
_____
_____
_____
_____
_____
_____
_____

Lodge: _____ **Date:** _____

Secretary & Treasurer Financial Reconciliation: *The Secretary and Treasurer will write a short summary*
of all funds received into the lodge by the Secretary and turned over to the Treasurer during the meeting in both books.

_____
_____
_____
_____
_____
_____
_____
_____
_____
_____
_____
_____
_____
_____
_____
_____
_____
_____
_____
_____
_____

Secretary's Signature: _____
Treasurers Signature: _____
Worshipful Masters Signature: _____

Audit Team Notes: _____
_____
_____
_____
_____
_____
_____
_____
_____
_____

Audit Team Signature: _____
Audit Team Signature: _____
Audit Team Signature: _____

Lodge: _____ **Date:** _____

21st Lodge Meeting

Time of Opening: _____

Roll Call of Officers   *List the present Officer, Assistant Officer Acting Officer (with "Acting" by their name) and Visiting Brothers names.*

Worshipful Master: _____
Senior Warden: _____
Junior Warden: _____
Secretary: _____
Treasurer: _____
Senior Deacon: _____
Junior Deacon: _____
Senior Steward: _____
Junior Steward: _____
Marshal: _____
Chaplain: _____
Tyler: _____

Visiting Brothers: _____
_____
_____
_____
_____
_____
_____
_____
_____
_____
_____
_____
_____
_____
_____
_____
_____
_____
_____
_____

Lodge: _____ **Date:** _____

Reading and Approval of Minutes: *Document finance related adjustments or corrections to the minutes.*

_____
_____
_____
_____
_____
_____
_____
_____
_____
_____
_____
_____
_____
_____
_____
_____
_____
_____

Treasurer Report: *In this section list the Previous Meeting Account Balance, Deposits Received, Account Debits, Current Account Balance, and Outstanding Checks.*

Current Account Balance: _____

_____
_____
_____
_____
_____
_____
_____
_____
_____
_____
_____
_____
_____
_____
_____
_____
_____
_____
_____

Lodge: _____   **Date:** _____

Funds Received: *In the section document all funds received from the Secretary and in what forms they were received. Example: 03 Checks: Check #'s 1123 for $100.00, 1134 for $250.00 and 2235 for $150.00, Total Checks $500.00. Total Cash Received: $250.00. Total Electronic Payments Received (verified in your service provider): $150.00. Grand Total Received: $900.00.*

Lodge: _____ **Date:** _____

Funds Received *(Continued)*: _____

_____
_____
_____
_____
_____
_____
_____
_____
_____
_____
_____
_____
_____
_____
_____
_____
_____
_____
_____
_____
_____
_____
_____
_____
_____
_____
_____
_____
_____
_____
_____
_____
_____
_____
_____
_____
_____
_____
_____

Lodge: _____ **Date:** _____

Funds Received *(Continued)*: _____

_____
_____
_____
_____
_____
_____
_____
_____
_____
_____
_____
_____
_____
_____
_____
_____
_____
_____
_____
_____
_____
_____
_____
_____
_____
_____
_____
_____
_____
_____
_____
_____
_____
_____
_____
_____
_____
_____
_____

Lodge: _____   **Date:** _____

Debits and Checks Dispersed: _Document all outgoing payments, the amount and method of_
disbursement as well as the receiver. (Including check and transaction numbers)

Lodge: _____ **Date:** _____

Debits and Checks Dispersed: *(Continued)* _____

_____
_____
_____
_____
_____
_____
_____
_____
_____
_____
_____
_____
_____
_____
_____
_____
_____
_____
_____
_____
_____
_____
_____
_____
_____
_____
_____
_____
_____
_____
_____
_____
_____
_____
_____
_____
_____
_____
_____
_____

Lodge: _____ **Date:** _____

Debits and Checks Dispersed: *(Continued)*

Lodge: _____   **Date:** _____

Reading of the Rough Minutes: *Document finance related adjustments or corrections to the minutes.*

_____
_____
_____
_____
_____
_____
_____
_____
_____
_____
_____
_____
_____
_____
_____
_____
_____
_____
_____

Treasurer Report: *In this section write a summary of financial transaction that transpired in the meeting. Example: Total funds received from the Secretary and Checks Written.*

Current Account Balance: _____

_____
_____
_____
_____
_____
_____
_____
_____
_____
_____
_____
_____
_____
_____
_____
_____
_____
_____

Lodge: _____ **Date:** _____

Notes: _____

_____
_____
_____
_____
_____
_____
_____
_____
_____
_____
_____
_____
_____
_____
_____
_____
_____
_____
_____
_____
_____
_____
_____
_____
_____
_____
_____
_____
_____
_____
_____
_____
_____
_____
_____
_____
_____
_____
_____
_____
_____

Lodge: _____ **Date:** _____

Notes: _____

_____

_____

_____

_____

_____

_____

_____

_____

_____

_____

_____

_____

_____

_____

_____

_____

_____

_____

_____

_____

_____

_____

_____

_____

_____

_____

_____

_____

_____

_____

_____

_____

_____

_____

_____

_____

_____

Lodge: _____ **Date:** _____

Secretary & Treasurer Financial Reconciliation: *The Secretary and Treasurer will write a short summary*
of all funds received into the lodge by the Secretary and turned over to the Treasurer during the meeting in both books.

_____
_____
_____
_____
_____
_____
_____
_____
_____
_____
_____
_____
_____
_____
_____
_____
_____
_____
_____
_____
_____
_____

Secretary's Signature: _____
Treasurers Signature: _____
Worshipful Masters Signature: _____

Audit Team Notes: _____
_____
_____
_____
_____
_____
_____
_____
_____
_____
_____

Audit Team Signature: _____
Audit Team Signature: _____
Audit Team Signature: _____

Lodge: _____   **Date:** _____

22nd Lodge Meeting

Time of Opening: _____

Roll Call of Officers   *List the present Officer, Assistant Officer Acting Officer (with "Acting" by their name) and Visiting Brothers names.*

Worshipful Master: _____
Senior Warden: _____
Junior Warden: _____
Secretary: _____
Treasurer: _____
Senior Deacon: _____
Junior Deacon: _____
Senior Steward: _____
Junior Steward: _____
Marshal: _____
Chaplain: _____
Tyler: _____

Visiting Brothers: _____
_____
_____
_____
_____
_____
_____
_____
_____
_____
_____
_____
_____
_____
_____
_____
_____
_____
_____
_____
_____
_____

Lodge: _____   **Date:** _____

Reading and Approval of Minutes: *Document finance related adjustments or corrections to the minutes.*

_____
_____
_____
_____
_____
_____
_____
_____
_____
_____
_____
_____
_____
_____
_____
_____
_____

Treasurer Report: *In this section list the Previous Meeting Account Balance, Deposits Received,*
Account Debits, Current Account Balance, and Outstanding Checks.

Current Account Balance: _____

_____
_____
_____
_____
_____
_____
_____
_____
_____
_____
_____
_____
_____
_____
_____
_____
_____
_____

Lodge: _____   **Date:** _____

Funds Received: _In the section document all funds received from the Secretary and in what forms they were received. Example: 03 Checks: Check #'s 1123 for $100.00, 1134 for $250.00 and 2235 for $150.00, Total Checks $500.00. Total Cash Received: $250.00. Total Electronic Payments Received (verified in your service provider): $150.00. Grand Total Received: $900.00._

_____
_____
_____
_____
_____
_____
_____
_____
_____
_____
_____
_____
_____
_____
_____
_____
_____
_____
_____
_____
_____
_____
_____
_____
_____
_____
_____
_____
_____
_____
_____
_____

Lodge: _____ **Date:** _____

Funds Received *(Continued):* _____

_____
_____
_____
_____
_____
_____
_____
_____
_____
_____
_____
_____
_____
_____
_____
_____
_____
_____
_____
_____
_____
_____
_____
_____
_____
_____
_____
_____
_____
_____
_____
_____
_____
_____
_____
_____
_____
_____
_____
_____
_____
_____
_____

Lodge: _____   **Date:** _____

Funds Received *(Continued)*: _____

_____
_____
_____
_____
_____
_____
_____
_____
_____
_____
_____
_____
_____
_____
_____
_____
_____
_____
_____
_____
_____
_____
_____
_____
_____
_____
_____
_____
_____
_____
_____
_____
_____
_____
_____
_____
_____
_____
_____
_____
_____
_____
_____
_____

Lodge: _____   **Date:** _____

Debits and Checks Dispersed: *Document all outgoing payments, the amount and method of*
disbursement as well as the receiver. (Including check and transaction numbers)

_____
_____
_____
_____
_____
_____
_____
_____
_____
_____
_____
_____
_____
_____
_____
_____
_____
_____
_____
_____
_____
_____
_____
_____
_____
_____
_____
_____
_____
_____
_____
_____
_____
_____
_____
_____
_____
_____
_____
_____
_____
_____

Lodge: _____ **Date:** _____

Debits and Checks Dispersed: *(Continued)* _____

Lodge: _____ **Date:** _____

Debits and Checks Dispersed: *(Continued)*

_____
_____
_____
_____
_____
_____
_____
_____
_____
_____
_____
_____
_____
_____
_____
_____
_____
_____
_____
_____
_____
_____
_____
_____
_____
_____
_____
_____
_____
_____
_____
_____
_____
_____
_____
_____
_____
_____

Lodge: _____   **Date:** _____

Reading of the Rough Minutes: *Document finance related adjustments or corrections to the minutes.*

_____
_____
_____
_____
_____
_____
_____
_____
_____
_____
_____
_____
_____
_____
_____
_____
_____
_____
_____

Treasurer Report: *In this section write a summary of financial transaction that transpired in the meeting. Example: Total funds received from the Secretary and Checks Written.*

Current Account Balance: _____

_____
_____
_____
_____
_____
_____
_____
_____
_____
_____
_____
_____
_____
_____
_____
_____
_____

Lodge: _____ **Date:** _____

Notes: _____

_____

_____

_____

_____

_____

_____

_____

_____

_____

_____

_____

_____

_____

_____

_____

_____

_____

_____

_____

_____

_____

_____

_____

_____

_____

_____

_____

_____

_____

_____

_____

_____

_____

_____

_____

_____

_____

_____

_____

_____

_____

_____

_____

Lodge: _____ **Date:** _____

Notes: _____

_____
_____
_____
_____
_____
_____
_____
_____
_____
_____
_____
_____
_____
_____
_____
_____
_____
_____
_____
_____
_____
_____
_____
_____
_____
_____
_____
_____
_____
_____
_____
_____
_____
_____
_____
_____
_____
_____
_____
_____
_____

Lodge: _____   **Date:** _____

Secretary & Treasurer Financial Reconciliation: *The Secretary and Treasurer will write a short summary*
of all funds received into the lodge by the Secretary and turned over to the Treasurer during the meeting in both books.

_____
_____
_____
_____
_____
_____
_____
_____
_____
_____
_____
_____
_____
_____
_____
_____
_____
_____
_____
_____
_____

Secretary's Signature: _____
Treasurers Signature: _____
Worshipful Masters Signature: _____

Audit Team Notes: _____
_____
_____
_____
_____
_____
_____
_____
_____
_____

Audit Team Signature: _____
Audit Team Signature: _____
Audit Team Signature: _____

Lodge: _____   **Date:** _____

23rd Lodge Meeting

Time of Opening: _____

Roll Call of Officers   *List the present Officer, Assistant Officer Acting Officer (with "Acting" by their name) and Visiting Brothers names.*

Worshipful Master: _____
Senior Warden: _____
Junior Warden: _____
Secretary: _____
Treasurer: _____
Senior Deacon: _____
Junior Deacon: _____
Senior Steward: _____
Junior Steward: _____
Marshal: _____
Chaplain: _____
Tyler: _____

Visiting Brothers: _____
_____
_____
_____
_____
_____
_____
_____
_____
_____
_____
_____
_____
_____
_____
_____
_____
_____
_____
_____
_____
_____

Lodge: _____ **Date:** _____

Reading and Approval of Minutes: _Document finance related adjustments or corrections to the minutes._

_____
_____
_____
_____
_____
_____
_____
_____
_____
_____
_____
_____
_____
_____
_____
_____
_____
_____

Treasurer Report: _In this section list the Previous Meeting Account Balance, Deposits Received, Account Debits, Current Account Balance, and Outstanding Checks._

Current Account Balance: _____

_____
_____
_____
_____
_____
_____
_____
_____
_____
_____
_____
_____
_____
_____
_____
_____
_____
_____
_____

Lodge: _____   **Date:** _____

Funds Received: *In the section document all funds received from the Secretary and in what forms they were received. Example: 03 Checks: Check #'s 1123 for $100.00, 1134 for $250.00 and 2235 for $150.00, Total Checks $500.00. Total Cash Received: $250.00. Total Electronic Payments Received (verified in your service provider): $150.00. Grand Total Received: $900.00.*

Lodge: _____ **Date:** _____

Funds Received *(Continued):* _____

_____
_____
_____
_____
_____
_____
_____
_____
_____
_____
_____
_____
_____
_____
_____
_____
_____
_____
_____
_____
_____
_____
_____
_____
_____
_____
_____
_____
_____
_____
_____
_____
_____
_____
_____
_____
_____
_____
_____
_____
_____
_____
_____
_____

Lodge: _____ **Date:** _____

Funds Received *(Continued)*: _____

_____
_____
_____
_____
_____
_____
_____
_____
_____
_____
_____
_____
_____
_____
_____
_____
_____
_____
_____
_____
_____
_____
_____
_____
_____
_____
_____
_____
_____
_____
_____
_____
_____
_____
_____
_____
_____
_____
_____

Lodge: _____ **Date:** _____

Debits and Checks Dispersed: _Document all outgoing payments, the amount and method of_
disbursement as well as the receiver. (Including check and transaction numbers)

Lodge: _____ **Date:** _____

Debits and Checks Dispersed: *(Continued)* _____

Lodge: _____ **Date:** _____

Debits and Checks Dispersed: *(Continued)*

_____
_____
_____
_____
_____
_____
_____
_____
_____
_____
_____
_____
_____
_____
_____
_____
_____
_____
_____
_____
_____
_____
_____
_____
_____
_____
_____
_____
_____
_____
_____
_____
_____
_____
_____
_____
_____
_____
_____

Lodge: _____   **Date:** _____

Reading of the Rough Minutes: _Document finance related adjustments or corrections to the minutes._

_____
_____
_____
_____
_____
_____
_____
_____
_____
_____
_____
_____
_____
_____
_____
_____
_____
_____

Treasurer Report: _In this section write a summary of financial transaction that transpired in the meeting. Example: Total funds received from the Secretary and Checks Written._

Current Account Balance: _____

_____
_____
_____
_____
_____
_____
_____
_____
_____
_____
_____
_____
_____
_____
_____
_____
_____

Lodge: _____   **Date:** _____

Notes: _____

_____
_____
_____
_____
_____
_____
_____
_____
_____
_____
_____
_____
_____
_____
_____
_____
_____
_____
_____
_____
_____
_____
_____
_____
_____
_____
_____
_____
_____
_____
_____
_____
_____
_____
_____
_____
_____
_____
_____
_____
_____
_____
_____
_____

Lodge: _____   **Date:** _____

Notes: _____

_____
_____
_____
_____
_____
_____
_____
_____
_____
_____
_____
_____
_____
_____
_____
_____
_____
_____
_____
_____
_____
_____
_____
_____
_____
_____
_____
_____
_____
_____
_____
_____
_____
_____
_____
_____
_____
_____
_____

Lodge: _____ **Date:** _____

Secretary & Treasurer Financial Reconciliation: *The Secretary and Treasurer will write a short summary*
of all funds received into the lodge by the Secretary and turned over to the Treasurer during the meeting in both books.

_____
_____
_____
_____
_____
_____
_____
_____
_____
_____
_____
_____
_____
_____
_____
_____
_____
_____
_____
_____

Secretary's Signature: _____

Treasurers Signature: _____

Worshipful Masters Signature: _____

Audit Team Notes: _____

_____
_____
_____
_____
_____
_____
_____
_____
_____

Audit Team Signature: _____

Audit Team Signature: _____

Audit Team Signature: _____

Lodge: _____   **Date:** _____

24ᵗʰ Lodge Meeting

Time of Opening: _____

Roll Call of Officers   *List the present Officer, Assistant Officer Acting Officer (with "Acting" by their name) and Visiting Brothers names.*

Worshipful Master: _____
Senior Warden: _____
Junior Warden: _____
Secretary: _____
Treasurer: _____
Senior Deacon: _____
Junior Deacon: _____
Senior Steward: _____
Junior Steward: _____
Marshal: _____
Chaplain: _____
Tyler: _____

Visiting Brothers: _____
_____
_____
_____
_____
_____
_____
_____
_____
_____
_____
_____
_____
_____
_____
_____
_____
_____
_____
_____

Lodge: _____ **Date:** _____

Reading and Approval of Minutes: *Document finance related adjustments or corrections to the minutes.*

_____
_____
_____
_____
_____
_____
_____
_____
_____
_____
_____
_____
_____
_____
_____
_____
_____
_____

Treasurer Report: *In this section list the Previous Meeting Account Balance, Deposits Received, Account Debits, Current Account Balance, and Outstanding Checks.*

Current Account Balance: _____

_____
_____
_____
_____
_____
_____
_____
_____
_____
_____
_____
_____
_____
_____
_____
_____
_____
_____

Lodge: _____   **Date:** _____

Funds Received: *In the section document all funds received from the Secretary and in what forms they were received. Example: 03 Checks: Check #'s 1123 for $100.00, 1134 for $250.00 and 2235 for $150.00, Total Checks $500.00. Total Cash Received: $250.00. Total Electronic Payments Received (verified in your service provider): $150.00. Grand Total Received: $900.00.*

Lodge: _____ **Date:** _____

Funds Received *(Continued):* _____

_____
_____
_____
_____
_____
_____
_____
_____
_____
_____
_____
_____
_____
_____
_____
_____
_____
_____
_____
_____
_____
_____
_____
_____
_____
_____
_____
_____
_____
_____
_____
_____
_____
_____
_____
_____
_____
_____
_____
_____
_____
_____
_____
_____
_____

Lodge: _____ **Date:** _____

Funds Received *(Continued)*: _____

_____
_____
_____
_____
_____
_____
_____
_____
_____
_____
_____
_____
_____
_____
_____
_____
_____
_____
_____
_____
_____
_____
_____
_____
_____
_____
_____
_____
_____
_____
_____
_____
_____
_____
_____
_____
_____
_____
_____

Lodge: _____ **Date:** _____

Debits and Checks Dispersed: _Document all outgoing payments, the amount and method of_
disbursement as well as the receiver. (Including check and transaction numbers)

Lodge: _____ **Date:** _____

Debits and Checks Dispersed: *(Continued)* _____

_____

_____

_____

_____

_____

_____

_____

_____

_____

_____

_____

_____

_____

_____

_____

_____

_____

_____

_____

_____

_____

_____

_____

_____

_____

_____

_____

_____

_____

_____

_____

_____

_____

_____

_____

_____

_____

_____

_____

_____

_____

_____

_____

_____

_____

_____

Lodge: _____ **Date:** _____

Debits and Checks Dispersed: *(Continued)*

_____
_____
_____
_____
_____
_____
_____
_____
_____
_____
_____
_____
_____
_____
_____
_____
_____
_____
_____
_____
_____
_____
_____
_____
_____
_____
_____
_____
_____
_____
_____
_____
_____
_____
_____
_____
_____
_____
_____
_____
_____

Lodge: _____   **Date:** _____

Reading of the Rough Minutes: *Document finance related adjustments or corrections to the minutes.*

_____
_____
_____
_____
_____
_____
_____
_____
_____
_____
_____
_____
_____
_____
_____
_____
_____
_____
_____

Treasurer Report: *In this section write a summary of financial transaction that transpired in the meeting. Example: Total funds received from the Secretary and Checks Written.*

Current Account Balance: _____

_____
_____
_____
_____
_____
_____
_____
_____
_____
_____
_____
_____
_____
_____
_____
_____
_____
_____

Lodge: _____ **Date:** _____

Notes: _____

_____
_____
_____
_____
_____
_____
_____
_____
_____
_____
_____
_____
_____
_____
_____
_____
_____
_____
_____
_____
_____
_____
_____
_____
_____
_____
_____
_____
_____
_____
_____
_____
_____
_____
_____
_____
_____
_____
_____

Lodge: _____   **Date:** _____

Notes: _____

_____

_____

_____

_____

_____

_____

_____

_____

_____

_____

_____

_____

_____

_____

_____

_____

_____

_____

_____

_____

_____

_____

_____

_____

_____

_____

_____

_____

_____

_____

_____

_____

_____

_____

_____

_____

_____

_____

_____

_____

_____

_____

_____

_____

Lodge: _____ **Date:** _____

Secretary & Treasurer Financial Reconciliation: *The Secretary and Treasurer will write a short summary*
of all funds received into the lodge by the Secretary and turned over to the Treasurer during the meeting in both books.

_____
_____
_____
_____
_____
_____
_____
_____
_____
_____
_____
_____
_____
_____
_____
_____
_____
_____
_____
_____

Secretary's Signature: _____
Treasurers Signature: _____
Worshipful Masters Signature: _____

Audit Team Notes: _____
_____
_____
_____
_____
_____
_____
_____
_____
_____
_____

Audit Team Signature: _____
Audit Team Signature: _____
Audit Team Signature: _____

Lodge: _____   **Date:** _____

_____ Lodge Meeting (Misc.)

Time of Opening: _____

Roll Call of Officers   *List the present Officer, Assistant Officer Acting Officer (with "Acting" by their name) and Visiting Brothers names.*

Worshipful Master: _____

Senior Warden: _____

Junior Warden: _____

Secretary: _____

Treasurer: _____

Senior Deacon: _____

Junior Deacon: _____

Senior Steward: _____

Junior Steward: _____

Marshal: _____

Chaplain: _____

Tyler: _____

Visiting Brothers: _____

_____

_____

_____

_____

_____

_____

_____

_____

_____

_____

_____

_____

_____

_____

_____

_____

_____

_____

_____

_____

Lodge: _____   **Date:** _____

Reading and Approval of Minutes: _Document finance related adjustments or corrections to the minutes._

_____
_____
_____
_____
_____
_____
_____
_____
_____
_____
_____
_____
_____
_____
_____
_____
_____

Treasurer Report: _In this section list the Previous Meeting Account Balance, Deposits Received, Account Debits, Current Account Balance, and Outstanding Checks._

Current Account Balance: _____

_____
_____
_____
_____
_____
_____
_____
_____
_____
_____
_____
_____
_____
_____
_____
_____
_____
_____

Lodge: _____   **Date:** _____

Funds Received: *In the section document all funds received from the Secretary and in what forms they were received. Example: 03 Checks: Check #'s 1123 for $100.00, 1134 for $250.00 and 2235 for $150.00, Total Checks $500.00. Total Cash Received: $250.00. Total Electronic Payments Received (verified in your service provider): $150.00. Grand Total Received: $900.00.*

_____

_____

_____

_____

_____

_____

_____

_____

_____

_____

_____

_____

_____

_____

_____

_____

_____

_____

_____

_____

_____

_____

_____

_____

_____

_____

_____

_____

_____

_____

_____

_____

_____

_____

_____

_____

_____

_____

_____

_____

Lodge: _____   **Date:** _____

Funds Received *(Continued)*: _____

_____
_____
_____
_____
_____
_____
_____
_____
_____
_____
_____
_____
_____
_____
_____
_____
_____
_____
_____
_____
_____
_____
_____
_____
_____
_____
_____
_____
_____
_____
_____
_____
_____
_____
_____
_____
_____
_____
_____
_____
_____
_____

Lodge: _____   **Date:** _____

Funds Received (*Continued*):   _____

_____

_____

_____

_____

_____

_____

_____

_____

_____

_____

_____

_____

_____

_____

_____

_____

_____

_____

_____

_____

_____

_____

_____

_____

_____

_____

_____

_____

_____

_____

_____

_____

_____

_____

_____

_____

_____

_____

_____

_____

_____

Lodge: _____   **Date:** _____

Debits and Checks Dispersed: _Document all outgoing payments, the amount and method of_
disbursement as well as the receiver. (Including check and transaction numbers)

_____

_____

_____

_____

_____

_____

_____

_____

_____

_____

_____

_____

_____

_____

_____

_____

_____

_____

_____

_____

_____

_____

_____

_____

_____

_____

_____

_____

_____

_____

_____

_____

_____

_____

_____

_____

_____

_____

_____

_____

_____

Lodge: _____   **Date:** _____

Debits and Checks Dispersed: *(Continued)*   _____

Lodge: _____ **Date:** _____

Debits and Checks Dispersed: *(Continued)*

Lodge: _____   **Date:** _____

Reading of the Rough Minutes: *Document finance related adjustments or corrections to the minutes.*

_____
_____
_____
_____
_____
_____
_____
_____
_____
_____
_____
_____
_____
_____
_____
_____
_____
_____

Treasurer Report: *In this section write a summary of financial transaction that transpired in the meeting. Example: Total funds received from the Secretary and Checks Written.*

Current Account Balance: _____

_____
_____
_____
_____
_____
_____
_____
_____
_____
_____
_____
_____
_____
_____
_____
_____
_____
_____

Lodge: _____ **Date:** _____

Notes: _____

_____

_____

_____

_____

_____

_____

_____

_____

_____

_____

_____

_____

_____

_____

_____

_____

_____

_____

_____

_____

_____

_____

_____

_____

_____

_____

_____

_____

_____

_____

_____

_____

_____

_____

_____

_____

_____

_____

_____

_____

_____

_____

_____

_____

_____

_____

_____

_____

_____

_____

Lodge: _____   **Date:** _____

Notes: _____

_____

_____

_____

_____

_____

_____

_____

_____

_____

_____

_____

_____

_____

_____

_____

_____

_____

_____

_____

_____

_____

_____

_____

_____

_____

_____

_____

_____

_____

_____

_____

_____

_____

_____

_____

_____

_____

_____

_____

Lodge: _____ **Date:** _____

Secretary & Treasurer Financial Reconciliation: *The Secretary and Treasurer will write a short summary* *of all funds received into the lodge by the Secretary and turned over to the Treasurer during the meeting in both books.*

_____
_____
_____
_____
_____
_____
_____
_____
_____
_____
_____
_____
_____
_____
_____
_____
_____
_____
_____
_____

Secretary's Signature: _____
Treasurers Signature: _____
Worshipful Masters Signature: _____

Audit Team Notes: _____
_____
_____
_____
_____
_____
_____
_____
_____
_____
_____
_____

Audit Team Signature: _____
Audit Team Signature: _____
Audit Team Signature: _____

Lodge: _____ **Date:** _____

Election of Officers

Document the results of elections for the oncoming year and the newly elected officers. Confirm the Brothers present is financial and within their rights to participate in elections.

Station	Nominee(s)	Tallies	Elected/Appointed
Worshipful Master			
Senior Warden			
Junior Warden			
Secretary			
Treasurer			
Senior Deacon			
Junior Deacon			
Senior Steward			
Junior Steward			

Lodge: _____ **Date:** _____

Election of Officers

Document the results of elections for the oncoming year and the newly elected officers. Confirm the Brothers present is financial and within their rights to participate in elections.

Station	Nominee(s)	Tallies	Elected
Tyler			
Chaplain			
Marshal			
Historian			
Master of Ceremony			
Lecturer/Ritualist			
Orator			
Almoner			

Lodge: _____   **Date:** _____

Election of Officers

Document the results of elections for the oncoming year and the newly elected officers.
Confirm the Brothers present is financial and within their rights to participate in elections.

Station	Nominee(s)	Tallies	Elected

Lodge: _____ **Date:** _____